MODEL GOVERNMENT CHARTERS

MODEL GOVERNMENT CHARTERS

A City, County, Regional, State, and Federal Handbook

EDITED BY ROGER L. KEMP

McFarland & Company, Inc., Publishers
Jefferson, North Carolina, and London

The present work is a reprint of the library bound edition of Model Government Charters: A City, County, Regional, State, and Federal Handbook, *first published in 2003 by McFarland.*

LIBRARY OF CONGRESS CATALOGUING-IN-PUBLICATION DATA

Model government charters : a city, county, regional, state, and
   federal handbook / edited by Roger L. Kemp.
      p.   cm.
   Includes bibliographical references and index.

   ISBN-13: 978-0-7864-3154-0
   (softcover : 50# alkaline paper) ∞

   1. Federal government — United States.   2. Local
government — United States.   3. Municipal government —
United States.   4. Charters.   I. Kemp, Roger L.
JK325.M63   2007
342.73'02 — dc21   2002154746

British Library cataloguing data are available

Cover photograph ©2007 Shutterstock

Manufactured in the United States of America

McFarland & Company, Inc., Publishers
   Box 611, Jefferson, North Carolina 28640
      www.mcfarlandpub.com

Contents

Preface

In 2002, the editor prepared a volume that described the state of American governments—city, county, regional, state, and federal—as they exist today. The title of this book was *How American Governments Work: A Handbook of City, County, Regional, State, and Federal Operations* (McFarland, 2002). The purpose of the present volume being to document and describe a set of *model* charters for each level of government in America, it serves as an excellent companion volume to that previous book since it describes *why* our nation's governments work (as opposed to *how*). Hence, this volume has been titled *Model Government Charters: A City, County, Regional, State, and Federal Handbook.*

The United States of America has the oldest system of federal government in the world. Since the passage of our federal constitution in 1789, the federal government has gained both power and responsibility. During this time, the states lost much of their original sovereignty given to them when the colonies were initially formed. Much of the shift of power to the federal government is attributable to Supreme Court Chief Justice John Marshall, during the early 18th century, and the federal policies arising from the New Deal of the 1930s, when the problems of the nation were too much for state governments to resolve on their own. This gradual shift of power has also had an influence on lower levels of government, since cities and counties are creatures of the states. Each state's charter and statutes determine the powers and responsibilities of these lower levels of government. Over the years, both the number and types of regional governments have grown in significance. Many of these new regional governments were

designed to address many of our nation's urban problems that spill over
the artificial man-made political boundaries of our cities and county governments. This level of government will continue to grow in the future.

The chapters included in this book, naturally, include the names
city, *county*, *regional*, *state*, and *federal*; followed by the word *government*.
Introductory chapters are included to familiarize the reader with each level
of government. A model charter follows each chapter. The word *charter* is
commonly used to describe the set of laws that forms cities, counties, and
regions. On the other hand, the term *constitution* is used when referring to
states and the federal government. For ease of reference, the term *charter*
denotes those sets of laws forming the basis of all levels of U.S. government. This volume also includes a *Glossary* of commonly used terms and
a *National Resource Directory*, which highlights major sources for further
research on those subjects contained in this volume. These topics, and the
types of information examined in each chapter, are briefly highlighted
below.

City Government

The four basic forms of municipal government in the U.S. include the
commission, council-manager, mayor-council, and strong mayor plans.
The commission plan involves the direct election of legislators who serve
as executives to manage the various functions of a municipal organization.
This form of government, which merges legislative and administrative
functions, because of its obvious shortcomings, remains in only a few small
towns in the northeastern portion of the nation. Under the mayor-council plan, the duties of the mayor vary greatly, depending upon the size of
the community. The mayor is also elected separately from the city council, and the duties of the mayor vary from municipality to municipality,
depending upon a community's charter. Our nation's larger cities are most
likely to have the strong mayor form of government. This plan has its obvious advantages and disadvantages, depending upon the qualifications and
character of the person selected to serve as mayor. As our nation enters
the 21st century, the council-manager plan is the most common form of
municipal government, and it is growing at a faster rate than any other
form of local government.

For this reason, the *model city charter* sets forth a structure of municipal government that separates policy-making from administration, and
insulates the personnel and finance functions from undue political influence.

The major topics examined in this charter include the powers of the city government, the role of the city council, and the duties of the city manager. The charter also includes a listing of all departments, offices, and agencies, and delineates in great detail the financial procedures and reporting requirements of the city government. Other important topics in the charter include election procedures, and provisions for citizen initiatives and referendums. This charter requires each community to have a Board of Ethics. Provisions are also included for future citizen changes to the charter, always by majority vote of the electorate. These provisions separate legislative and executive powers, and are non-partisan in nature, allowing the appointed professional manager to serve all citizens equally, regardless of their political affiliation.

County Government

There are three primary types of county government in our nation. They include the commission, council-manager, and the council-elected executive plans. The commission plan allows for the direct election of legislators-administrators, who individually manage the various functions of county government. As with cities, this form of government has declined in popularity over the years, and is seldom used today. Under the council-elected executive plan, the county executive is directly elected by voters and serves as the top administrator of the county government. This plan can also be good or bad, depending upon the qualifications and character of the person selected to serve as the elected executive. The current trend, like in cities and towns, is towards the council-manager plan. It is the fastest growing form of county government in the country. Under this plan the elected county council appoints the council manager, who is a trained professional. County governments also have some elected department managers, depending the requirements of their charter. As is the case with the municipal council-manager plan, this form of government separates policy-making from administration, and insulates the personnel and finance functions of county government from undue political influence. In many county governments, the word "administrator" is used rather than the term "manager."

The *model county charter* mandates the council-manager plan because of its obvious advantages over the other forms of county government. The topics examined in this charter include the powers of the county government, the role of the county council, and the duties of the county manager (or administrator). This charter also includes a listing of all departments, offices, and agencies, and sets forth with specificity the financial procedures and reporting requirements of the county government. Other significant provisions in this charter include provisions for county elections, and requirements for citizen-initiated initiatives and referendums. This charter also requires each county under this plan to have a Board of Ethics. Provisions also contain a process whereby citizens can change their county charter by majority vote. This charter, like the city charter, incorporates the corporate model of governance [with a chairman and board of directors (chairman and council), a chief executive officer (county manager), and stockholders (citizens)].

Regional Government

There are six main forms of regional governments in the United States. These include regional planning commissions, councils of government, regional advisory committees, regional allocation agencies, special purpose regional agencies, and home-rule charter regional governments. Regional planning commissions may encompass a single county, multiple counties, multiple municipal jurisdictions, or some combination thereof. Councils of government usually include a number of neighboring cities, contiguous cities and the county they are located in, or adjacent cities and multiple neighboring counties. Regional advisory committees are created by states to oversee the planning function of portions of land within their jurisdiction. Regional allocation agencies are typically responsible for allocating certain federal funds within selected geographic areas, usually substrate in nature. Special purpose regional agencies have the authority to plan and control development in a selected portion of a state. Home-rule charter regional governments are few and far between. While there are some county-city consolidations, and a few state-created regional governments, there is only one regional government in America that has a home-rule charter, and public officials elected by the citizens within the region. This is the Metropolitan Services District in Portland, Oregon. The number of such regional governments will increase in popularity during the coming decades.

For this reason, the citizen-approved charter for this regional planning agency serves as the *model regional government charter* featured in this chapter. The charter for the nation's only home-rule regional government includes provisions that define its name and political boundaries; functions and powers; finances and revenues; form of government; its offices, commissions, and employees; provisions for elections and reapportionment, and power to enact laws (called ordinances). Reapportionment takes place after an "official" government census. The form of government includes the election of a seven (7)-member council, with one member being elected at-large to serve as president of the Metropolitan Council. The president and members of the council all serve four (4) year terms-of-office. Voters approved the Metropolitan Services District in 1992. Prior to 1992, the Oregon State Legislature set forth their legal obligations and responsibilities. It is considered by experts as one of the most progressive regional government organizations in the country. The "Metro," as locals usually refer to it, serves over 1.3 million people in a three (3) county area that contains twenty-four (24) cities in the Portland, Oregon, metropolitan area.

State Government

Our nation was founded with 13 colonies. When the Founding Fathers wrote the U.S. Constitution in 1787, these colonies became the first states in America. The Founding Fathers believed that more states would want to join the Union in the future, and that each state should have similar powers and structure. Even when the 50th state joined the Union, all states maintained these original characteristics. Each state's government is based on a constitution, and has a republican form of government. No state constitution is allowed to contradict the federal constitution, and each state has three branches of government. These three branches of government include the legislative, executive, and judicial, complete with their separation-of-powers and requirements for checks-and-balances. Most states provide citizens with one or more avenues of direct democracy — the initiative, referendum, or recall. Over the decades, power has shifted from the states to the federal government, especially during times of crisis. The current trend towards the devolution of responsibilities from the federal government to the states is restoring legitimate power to state governments. This trend is significant as our nation enters the third millennium, and likely to continue in the future.

The authority, structure, and responsibilities for each state are embodied in the *model state government charter* (or constitution). The structure of every state government includes provisions for a legislative, judicial, and executive branch of government. This model constitution includes a bill of rights, setting forth the rights of citizens; the powers of the state; and the qualifications to vote and how elections will be held. The roles and responsibilities for the state legislature, executive (governor), and judiciary (court system) are also set forth. The powers of the state to raise revenues and finance government are also established. The organization of local governments (cities and counties) are also included, along with the requirements for municipal and county elections. Lastly, this constitution includes civil service safeguards and defines and supports intergovernmental relations. Last, but not least, guidelines are mandated for ways that legislators and citizens can make revisions to their state constitution. The model state constitution clearly sets forth the structure, authority, and responsibilities for the required three (3) levels of state government, and their respective checks-and-balances.

Federal Government

The U.S. Constitution, the charter of the federal government, defines, directly or indirectly, the structure and responsibilities of our central government. According to the Constitution, any power not specifically given to the federal government is a power of the states or of the people. The country has changed tremendously since 1787 when the Founding Fathers wrote the original charter. Changing circumstances over the years have made it necessary to amend or change the Constitution and to expand the role of the federal government in our intergovernmental system. The original philosophy and concepts contained in the Constitution, however, have not changed over the years even though the federal government has grown in both size and complexity. Political scholars have long recognized the importance of early Supreme Court decisions, primarily during the first quarter of the 18th century, as well as the federal government's policies of the New Deal, during the second quarter of the 19th century, as pivotal periods in redefining the role of the federal government in our nation. The role of the federal government continues to evolve as our nation enters the next century.

The Constitution, our nation's first charter, includes three parts. Part one includes the original charter, and its seven Articles that set forth the organization of the U.S. government, our national election processes, and our government's inherent system of checks-and-balances that still exists today. Part two, called the Bill of Rights, includes Amendments 1 through 10 of the Constitution, which set forth the basic rights of citizens, and the numerous safeguards that exist to ensure these rights. The first 10 Amendments were adopted as a unit in 1791. Part three of the Constitution includes some 27 Amendments to the Constitution that were ratified during the ensuing two-plus centuries. Amendment 1 was passed in 1798, and Amendment 27 was approved in 1992. Relative to states' rights, the most important of these Amendments is the 14th, which was ratified in 1868. This Amendment placed significant limitations on the powers of the states. It extended the federal protections of the Bill of Rights to citizens under state law, who previously had to look to each state constitution for such rights. The other provision of the 14th Amendment places limits upon the powers of the state and is the guarantee of "equal protection under the law" for all citizens of the United States. The Supreme Court applied this clause in its landmark decision outlawing school segregation (*Brown v. Board of Education of Topeka*, 1954).

The final two sections of this reference volume include a *Glossary* and a *National Resource Directory*. The *Glossary* includes definitions to about 125 terms commonly used to describe city, county, regional, state, and federal governments, including the actions taken by their public officials. The *National Resource Directory* includes a listing of some 24 major national professional associations and research organizations serving city, county, regional, state, and federal government. Many of these organizations are membership organizations. This listing includes the name of each organization, along with its mailing address, telephone number, FAX number, and internet address. Before contacting any of these organizations, the reader is encouraged to review the material available over the internet for each of these organizations. In many cases, a wealth of information is available over the internet, including the history of these organizations, and a listing of their current programs and activities, including membership requirements (if appropriate). Frequently, publications may also be ordered over the internet directly from these organizations. Most of these websites will accept direct e-mail inquiries from the public.

The main purpose of this book is to document those government charters that form the basis of each level of government in America in the early 21st century. After all, the state of our democratic institutions—at all levels of government—is dependent upon the written laws that form the very essence of their existence. Citizens and public officials alike should find this volume useful for a number of reasons. Citizens wishing to improve any level of their government now have access to a set of *model charters* that show the best practices for each level of government. These include forms of organization, election systems, personnel practices, and financial safeguards and reporting requirements, and provisions for direct democracy, such as the initiative, referendum, and recall. Public officials also need this type of information as they strive to improve the operations of their own governments to meet the expectations of the citizens they serve. Equally as important, as new cities are formed in the unincorporated areas of our nation's counties, citizens and public officials alike can reference the model municipal charter. This also holds true for new regional governments that may be formed in the years ahead. A model charter now exists that can provide guidelines for similar government agencies.

Most published works of this nature only focus on a single level of government. This is the only volume known to set forth model charters for every level of American government. For this reason, it represents an important codification of knowledge in this field.

Roger L. Kemp
Meriden, Connecticut
Spring 2003

1

City Government

Roger L. Kemp

Businessmen have been convinced for many years that professional managers are essential to their organizations. Professional managers are trained for their jobs through formal education and experience. The professional manager uses analytical skills to solve business problems in the best long-term interests of the company, and is guided by a code of professional ethics that avoids conflicts-of-interest. These attributes apply both to business managers and to the managers of local government.[1]

Business firms spend substantial amounts of money for training and educational programs to foster the development of their professional managers. Unfortunately, the need for professional managers and their continuing development and training is not always recognized in local governments.[2] Certainly, city governments are big businesses. Usually, they are the largest employers in the city, have expenditure levels comparable to large private sector companies, and have borrowings of an equal scale.

We want our city governments to be run by our elected representatives. Because of this, we frequently have difficulty reconciling the need for professional management with the role of the elected officials. The council-manager form of government provides the best answer to effective leadership by the mayor and city council, and a professional approach to solving the city's problems. The record of American cities and their accomplishments attests to this form of government.[3]

This chapter will set forth the different forms of local government in the United States, outline the history of the council-manager form of municipal government, including its success and popularity, examine the duties of a typical city manager, and analyze the factors that should be taken into consideration before implementing a desirable plan to manage a city — regardless of what form it takes. Any plan of government, naturally, should be in keeping with the wishes of the people as expressed through their publicly elected representatives.

Different Forms of Local Government

There are several workable forms of local government. They usually depend upon the role of the central government, and the degree of home-rule powers given to cities in running the affairs of communities. The typical types of local governments in the United States include strong mayor, commission, mayor-council, and council-manager plans. The characteristics of each are highlighted below.

Strong Mayor. In many large cities in America, the mayor is elected to "lead" the city. This typically includes running the municipal organization through city employees, with the top management being selected by the mayor. This plan has its obvious advantages and disadvantages, depending upon the qualifications of the person elected as the mayor. A good political leader is sometimes not a good municipal administrator. Hiring trained administrators has served to overcome this shortcoming.[4]

Commission. This form of government, which usually employs non-partisan, at-large elections, includes a board of commissioners. Collectively they serve as the legislative body. Individually, each commissioner serves as the head of one or more administrative departments. The municipal reform movement in the United States has all but led to the demise of this type of local government. Its weaknesses are obvious, since few elected leaders possess the necessary requirements to operate large portions of a municipal organization.[5]

Mayor-Council. This form has a legislative body that is elected either at-large, by ward or district, or by some combination of the two (e.g., some at-large and others by district). The distinguishing characteristics of this plan are two. One, the mayor is elected separately, and two, the official designation of the Office of the Mayor is the formal head of the city government. Depending upon local laws, the powers of the mayor may vary greatly, from limited ceremonial duties to full-scale authority to appoint and remove department managers. The mayor sometimes has veto power over the city council.[6]

Council-Manager. This form of government has a legislative body elected by popular vote. They are responsible for policymaking, while the management of the organization is under the direction of a city manager. The council appoints and removes the manager by majority vote. The mayor is a member of the council, with no special veto or administrative powers. The mayor is, however, the community's recognized political leader and represents the city at official ceremonies, as well as civic and social functions.[7]

The strong mayor form is limited to some large cities in most states. It is seldom the form used in small and medium-sized communities. The commission plan, while still in existence in a few cities in selected states, is not in widespread use. Because of its inherent limitations, it is not perceived as a model of municipal organization. The mayor-council plan exists primarily in larger cities. The city manager, or chief administrative officer, is appointed by the entire city council. The duties of the administrator vary from city to city. This plan works well when implemented properly, but is not increasing in number among local governments.[8]

The council-manager plan, the topic of this chapter, is the most successful and popular model of local government in most communities across America. Some facts about this plan are summarized below.

- Over 3,000 cities in the United States operate under this plan.
- Over 80 percent of cities recognized by the International City Management Association operate under this form of government.
- It is the single most popular form of government in cities over 10,000 in population.
- Dade County, Florida is the largest council-manager jurisdiction in the United States.
- Larger council-manager cities in America include Dallas, Texas; San Diego, California; San Jose, California; Miami, Florida; and Cincinnati, Ohio.
- Over 80 counties in the United States operate under this plan.
- This form of government represents over 100 million citizens in America.
- The council-manager plan is adopted more than once each week by a city or county, on the average, since 1945 (75 local governments adopt this plan each year).

• This form of government is growing faster than any other form of local government because of its popularity.

The council-manager form of government is the fastest growing form of government in the United States. Since 1984, the council-manager plan has grown by over 13 percent, while other forms of local government have decreased throughout the U.S. These national trends are documented in Figures 1-1 and 1-2.

History and Growth of the Council-Manager Plan

The council-manager plan of local government has been called one of the few original American contributions to political theory. Half a century after the first city manager experiment in Staunton, Virginia, one out of four Americans lives in a city organized under this plan, and nearly 2,500 in the United States are run by city managers, with the political leadership and policy making being provided by locally elected representatives. The council-manager plan was a product of the Progressive reform

---

Figure 1-1
Council-Manager Government:
The Fastest Growing Form of U.S. Local Government Structure

Form of Government	2000	1998	1996	1992	1988	1984
Council-Manager	3,302 (48.3%)	3,232	2,760	2,441	2,356	2,290 (34.7%)
Mayor-Council	2,988 (43.7%)	2,943	3,319	3,635	3,686	3,686 (55.8%)
Commission	143 (2.1%)	146	154	168	173	176 (2.7%)
Town Meeting	334 (4.9%)	333	365	363	369	370 (5.6%)
Representative Town Meeting	65 (1.0%)	65	70	79	82	81 (1.2%)
Total	6,832[1] (100%)	6,719[1]	6,668[1]	6,686[1]	6,666[1]	6,603[1] (100%)

[1]Totals for U.S. local governments represent those municipalities with populations of 2,500 and greater. There are close to 30,000 additional local governments with populations of less than 2,500. Only those that have been recognized by ICMA as having a professional manager or administrator are included in the Association's database; therefore, municipalities with populations of less than 2,500 have not been included in this calculation.

Source: The Municipal Year Books *1984–2000, published by the International City/County Management Association (ICMA), Washington, D.C.*

Figure 1-2
Council-manager Fast Facts

- More than 75.5 million individuals live in communities operating under council-manager governments.
- During the past 16 years, an average of 63 U.S. communities per year have adopted the council-manager form.
- Sixty-three percent of U.S. cities with populations of 25,000 or more have adopted the council-manager form.
- Fifty-seven percent of U.S. cities with populations of 10,000 or more have adopted the council-manager form.
- Fifty-three percent of U.S. cities with populations of 5,000 or more have adopted the council-manager form.

  Source: William H. Hansell, "Evolution and Change Characterize Council-Manager Government," *Public Management*, Vol. 82, No. 8, August, 2000, published by the International City-County Management Association, Washington, D.C.

---

era in local politics and is now three-quarters of a century old. The various factors leading to the growth and popularity of this form of municipal government are examined in the following paragraphs.

While the plan developed slowly, it was the product of several ideas and forces that shaped political management thought in America. Among those factors that affected its development most significantly were the growth of urbanization, the popularity of business and corporate ideals, the Progressive reform movement, and the professional public administration movement. These ideological and social roots of the council-manager plan are highlighted below.

Growth of Urbanization. Urbanization at the turn of the century dramatically changed the landscape of cities across the nation. During this time, towns and cities experienced rapid growth. While the rural population doubled, the urban population grew seven times its previous size. Urbanization quickly converted villages to towns, towns into cities, and cities into metropolitan centers. The rise of cities during this era was attributable to numerous social and economic forces, including the decline of agricultural industry, the rise of modern industries, the expansion of the economy generally, positive governmental and financial incentives for industrial growth, and a massive influx of overseas immigrants. Urbanization placed unprecedented demands on local governments throughout the country for additional public facilities and services. These factors led to the need for specialized expertise to manage the various facets of local governments.[9]

Popularity of Business and Corporate Ideals. Businessmen and the public concept of the corporation have been instrumental in determining public values. The success of corporations in the private sector had a significant influence on American political and administrative thought. Probably no political or administrative philosophy reflects business practices and corporate ideals more clearly than the growth of the council-manager plan. Many citizens still compare the operation of local government with that of the private corporation. The elected representatives are the board of directors, the city manager is the general manager, and the citizens of the community are the stockholders of the government.[10] Economy and efficiency, two primary values of the business community, are foundations of the council-manager plan.[11]

Progressive Reform Movement. Many of the effects of rapid urbanization, particularly the early political machines and large monopolistic corporations, met with disfavor among many citizens, who were known as Progressives. These individuals, who formed a significant movement because of their large numbers, felt that the best interests of the public were frequently not being served by the existing political processes and some large corporations that were perceived as being too strong and having too much power over common people. One of the most significant municipal reforms developed and supported by the Progressives was the council-manager plan. The management concepts embodied in this plan ideally suited the Progressive political philosophy of the time — a competent professional manager and public policy established by nonpartisan elected representatives. The manager's apolitical qualities suited the Progressive values, which favored impartiality and looked down upon personality politics and favoritism. Two key Progressive ideals, equality of participation in the political process and centralized administrative authority, were well balanced in the council-manager plan.[12]

Public Administration Movement. The modern city management profession also fits with the emerging "modern" concepts of public management in the early 1900s. Many administrative scholars espoused a sharp division between policy determination and policy implementation. Many scholars of the time drew a sharp distinction between "politics" and "administration."[13] The council-manager plan incorporated the ideals of the separation of policymaking and the implementation of public policy. The elected representatives are responsible for setting public policy; the city manager is concerned with its implementation. The separation of these two tasks formed the basis of the emerging council-manager form of local government.[14]

As the Progressive movement emerged and spread, the public administration thought of the time, together with the growth of urbanization, and the increasing popularity of business and corporate ideals, provided the positive background against which the council-manager plan blossomed into national popularity. All of these ideological and social forces provided the positive environment in which the council-manager plan spread from city to city across the landscape of America's local governments.

The City Manager's Role

The council-manager plan emphasizes the separation of the roles of policymaking and the administration of operating a city. The public officials, elected by the people, set the policy of the municipal organization. The city manager, appointed by the elected officials, is responsible for the implementation of the policy, as well as running the daily duties of the ongoing organization. The city manager is solely responsible to the elected representatives, and can normally be terminated at will if he or she does not perform the job properly. The typical duties of the city manager include, but are not limited to, the following tasks[15]:

- The administration of the management affairs of the city.
- Appointing and removing (for cause) all employees of the municipal organization.
- All employees, including the management staff, are hired based on their professional qualifications and experience in municipal affairs.
- Preparation, along with the financial staff, of the annual budget. While the budget is approved by the elected officials, it is implemented by the management staff.
- Keeping the elected officials informed about the financial condition of the city, including revenue and expenditure projections.
- Recommends salary and pay schedules for each appointive position. While competitive salaries and wages are desirable, the ability to pay also enters into the picture.
- In addition to implementing policies, the city manager makes policy recommendations to the elected officials consistent with sound management practices.

- Recommends the organizational structure, all reorganizations and consolidations, for the efficient and effective operation of the municipal organization.
- Attends all meetings of the city council, except when excused in advance. The manager is also required to advertise and post public notices of all such meetings.
- Supervises the acquisition of all materials, supplies, and equipment that are in the approved budget. The manager also supervises the awarding of all contracts for services within the amounts specified by the elected officials.
- All contracts above a specified amount are subject to competitive bidding procedures, usually by receiving "sealed" bids by a specified date. Contracts are awarded to the lowest responsible bidder.
- When services or contracts are necessary, and not in the approved budget, an additional approval is needed from the elected officials prior to awarding the contract.
- Rules governing the purchase of goods and services, and the awarding of contracts, are normally recommended by the city manager and approved by the elected officials. All such policies must be consistent with applicable laws.
- The city manager ensures that all laws and policies approved by the elected officials are enforced equally throughout the city. Old and outdated laws are periodically revised or eliminated as appropriate.
- Investigates all citizen complaints, and problems in the administrative organization. The manager recommends changes, as necessary, to the elected officials for their approval.
- The city manager is required to devote his or her entire time to the discharge of all official duties. Any outside employment is usually approved in advance by the elected representatives to ensure that no conflict-of-interest exists.

The Future of the Council-Manager Plan

There are several different forms of governmental structure that cities can adopt including, among others, the strong mayor form, the commission type, the mayor-council plan, as well as the council-manager model. Each structure's strengths and weaknesses lie in the eyes of the constituent, the political office holder, the professional government manager, or the employees of the municipal organization. The particular form to select is not an easy decision to make. Certainly, elected leaders, above all, want to be responsive to their constituents. For many communities in America, the council-manager plan has a proven track record of success.

Nearly 2,500 cities in the United States operate under the traditional council-manager plan, with its separation between the policy-making role of elected officials and the implementation of the policy being left to the professional government manager. This is the most successful and popular form of government in cities over 10,000 in population. Some of the larger cities in America have also been successful in implementing the council-manager plan. The fact that this form of government has been adopted on the average of once each week by a city or county in the United States since 1945 attests to the desirability of this model of municipal government representation. Because of its popularity among citizens, it is the fastest growing form of local government in America.

The form of local government a city selects should best serve the needs of the people. Voters elect their representatives, based on their confidence, not only to set public policies, but also to see to it that policies are implemented into programs and services to serve the community. If the council-manager plan best serves this goal, it may be the most desirable form of local government. If another form of governmental structure is utilized, be it the strong mayor form, the commission type, the mayor-council model, or some other combination of these, it should embody the representational needs of citizens. The form of government best suited for a particular city should be determined through the electoral process. No system of government is perfect, nor can any single system represent the wishes of all of the people all of the time. When the form of local government selected represents the wishes of the majority of the people, this is the form that best serves the democratic process and the will of the people.

Some facts about the council-manager plan over the past century of American history, the country's most popular form of municipal government, are highlighted below in Figure 1-3.

For nearly a century, the council-manager plan has been successfully modified and adapted to fit the needs of those citizens that live in America's communities. Cities and towns are not static, and the changes taking place in them involve the very core of the values held by society concerning how to govern where they live. Professional managers and the council-manager plan continue to evolve so that in contemporary times

---

Figure 1-3
Council-Manager Facts

For the past 86 years, the choice of U.S. communities has been council-manager government. Since the early 1900s, the council-manager form has become the most popular system of local government for communities with populations of 5,000 or more.

By 1918, there were 98 council-manager localities; in 1930, ICMA recognized 418 U.S. cities and seven counties as operating under the council-manager form. And by 1985, the number of council-manager communities had grown to 548 cities and 86 counties in the United States. Currently, 3,302 U.S. cities with populations greater than 2,500 and 371 U.S. counties operate under this system of local government.[16]

---

this plan offers the majority of citizens the municipal government they are seeking to satisfy their expectations of an effective local governance structure.

The council-manager plan continues to serve the needs of American communities in the 21st century. Today, more than 75 million citizens live and work in council-manager communities. For this reason, this system of municipal government continues to be the most popular form of local government in American history. This model of government provides the most effective organizational structure for citizen-public official accountability for the many cities and towns throughout our nation.

This form reflects the will of the people, and citizens continue to adopt this form of government in great numbers, since it embodies the coveted private sector corporate model (with the chairman of the board, the board of directors, the chief executive officer, and the corporation's stockholders). This translates into an elected mayor and city council (the chairman of the board and the board of directors), which serve as policy makers who serve the citizens (i.e., stockholders) of the community (the municipal corporation). The city manager is the chief executive officer, who reports to the board of directors.

This organizational model, the darling of the private sector for over a century, is coveted by citizens as the most desired system to overlay on their municipal government. This system provides citizens with the type of local government they desire as educated electors of our society.

MODEL CITY GOVERNMENT CHARTER
Christopher T. Gates

Article I
POWERS OF THE CITY

Section 1.01. Powers of the City.
The city shall have all powers possible for a city to have under the constitution and laws of this state as fully and completely as though they were specifically enumerated in this charter.

Section 1.02. Construction.
The powers of the city under this charter shall be construed liberally in favor of the city, and the specific mention of particular powers in the charter shall not be construed as limiting in any way the general power granted in this article.

Section 1.03. Intergovernmental Relations.
The city may exercise any of its powers or perform any of its functions and may participate in the financing thereof, jointly or in cooperation, by contract or otherwise, with any one or more states or any state civil division or agency, or the United States or any of its agencies.

Article II
CITY COUNCIL

Section 2.01. General Powers and Duties.
All powers of the city shall be vested in the city council, except as otherwise provided by law or this charter, and the council shall provide for the exercise thereof and for the performance of all duties and obligations imposed on the city by law.

Section 2.02. Composition, Eligibility, Election and Terms.

Alternative I: Election At-Large

Form 1

NOTE: This formulation of the at-large council system should be used

with the separately elected mayor form of the Council-Manager plan, as found in Alternative I of §2.03. The formulation for use with the form of the Council-Manager plan where the mayor is elected by the council from its membership is found in Form 2.

(a) **Composition.** There shall be a city council composed of the mayor and [even-number] members; the council members shall be elected by the voters of the city at large and the mayor shall be elected as provided in §2.03.

(b) **Eligibility.** Only registered voters of the city shall be eligible to hold the office of council member or mayor.

(c) **Election and Terms.** The regular election of council members shall be held on the _____ of _____ in each odd- [even-] numbered year, in the manner provided by law. At the first election under this charter _____ council members shall be elected; the _____ [one-half the number of council members] candidates receiving the greatest number of votes shall serve for terms of four years, and the _____ [one-half the number of council members] candidates receiving the next greatest number of votes shall serve for terms of two years. Thereafter, all council members shall be elected for four-year terms. The terms of council members shall begin the _____ day of _____ after their election.

NOTE: If staggered terms are not desired, use the following section:

[(c) **Election and Terms.** The regular election of council members shall be held on the _____ day of _____ every _____ years beginning in _____. The terms of council members shall be _____ years beginning the _____ day of _____ after their election.]

Form 2

NOTE: This formulation of the at-large council system should be used with the form of the Council-Manager plan where the mayor is elected by the council from its membership, as found in Alternative II of §2.03. The formulation for use with the separately elected mayor form of the Council-Manager plan is found in Form 1.

(a) **Composition.** There shall be a city council of [odd-number] members elected by the voters of the city at large.

(b) **Eligibility.** Only registered voters of the city shall be eligible to hold the office of council member.

(c) **Election and Terms.** The regular election of council members shall be held on the _____ of _____ in each odd- [even-] numbered year, in the manner provided by law. At the first election under this charter _____ council members shall be elected; the _____ [one-half plus one] candidates receiving the greatest number of votes shall serve for terms of four years, and the _____ [remainder of the council] candidates receiving the next greatest number of votes shall serve for terms of two years. Commencing at the next regular election and at all subsequent elections, all council members shall be elected for four-year terms. The terms of council members shall begin the _____ day of _____ after their election.

NOTE: If staggered terms are not desired, use the following section:

[(c) **Election and Terms.** The regular election of council members shall be held on the _____ day of _____ every _____ years beginning in _____. The terms of council members shall be _____ years beginning the _____ day of _____ after their election.]

**Alternative II:
Election At Large with
District Residency Requirement**

Form 1

NOTE: This formulation of the at-large council system with district residency requirements should be used with the separately elected mayor form of the Council-Manager plan, as found in Alternative I of §2.03. The formulation for use with the form of the Council-Manager plan where the mayor is elected by the council from its membership is found in Form 2.

(a) **Composition.** There shall be a city council composed of the mayor and [even-number] council members. Not more than one council member shall reside in each of the [even-number] districts provided for in Article VI; all shall be nominated and elected by the voters of the city at large. The mayor shall be elected in accordance with the provision of §2.03.

(b) **Eligibility.** Only registered voters of the city shall be eligible to hold the office of council member or mayor.

(c) **Election and Terms.** The regular election of council members shall be held on the _____ of _____ in each odd- [even-] numbered year, in the manner provided by law. At the first election under this charter _____ council members shall be elected; council members from odd-numbered districts shall serve for terms of two years, and council members from even-numbered districts shall serve for terms of four years. Thereafter, all council members shall serve for terms of four years. The terms of council members shall begin the _____ day of _____ after their election.

NOTE: If staggered terms are not desired, use the following section:

[(c) **Election and Terms.** The regular election of council members shall be held on the _____ day of _____ every _____ years beginning in _____. The terms of council members shall be _____ years beginning the _____ day of _____ after their election.]

Form 2

NOTE: This formulation of the at-large council system with district residence requirements should be used with the form of the Council-Manager plan where the mayor is elected by the council from its membership, as found in Alternative II of §2.03. The formulation for use with the separately elected mayor form of the Council-Manager plan is found in Form 1.

(a) **Composition.** There shall be a city council of [odd-number] members; not more than one shall reside in each of the [odd-number] districts provided for in Article VI. All shall be nominated and elected by the voters of the city at large.

(b) **Eligibility.** Only registered voters of the city shall be eligible to hold the office of council member.

(c) **Election and Terms.** The regular election of council members shall be held on the _____ of _____ in each odd- [even-] numbered year, in the manner provided by law. At the first election under this charter _____ council members shall be elected; the _____ candidates receiving the greatest number of votes shall serve for terms of four years, and the _____ candidates receiving the next greatest number of votes shall serve for terms of two years. Thereafter, all council members shall be elected for four-year terms. The terms of council members shall begin the _____ day of _____ after their election.

NOTE: If staggered terms are not desired, use the following section.

[(c) **Election and Terms.** The regular election of council members shall be held on the _____ day of _____ every _____ years beginning in _____.

The terms of council members shall be _____ years beginning the _____ day of _____ after their election.]

Alternative III: Mixed At-Large and Single Member District System

Form 1

NOTE: This formulation of the mixed at-large and single-member district system should be used with Alternative I of §2.03.

(a) **Composition.** There shall be a city council composed of the mayor and [even-number] members. _____ council members shall be nominated and elected by the voters of the city at large, and _____ shall be nominated and elected by the voters of each of the _____ council districts, as provided in Article VI. The mayor shall be elected as provided in §2.02.

(b) **Eligibility.** Only registered voters of the city shall be eligible to hold the office of council member.

(c) **Election and Terms.** The terms of council members shall be _____ years beginning the _____ day of _____ after their election.

Form 2

NOTE: When this formulation of the mixed at-large and single-member district system is used with Alternative II of §2.03 (the form of the Council-Manager plan where the mayor is selected by the council from its membership), it should specify in §2.03 that one of the at-large members shall be designated mayor.

(a) **Composition.** There shall be a city council of [odd-number] members. _____ shall be nominated and elected by the voters of the city at large, and _____ shall be nominated and elected by the voters of each of the _____ council districts, as provided in Article VI.

(b) **Eligibility.** Only registered voters of the city shall be eligible to hold the office of council member.

(c) **Election and Terms.** The terms of council members shall be _____ years beginning the _____ day of _____ after their election.

Alternative IV:
Single-Member District System

NOTE: The single-member district system should be used only where the mayor is elected at large as provided in Alternative I of §2.03 and not where the mayor is elected by and from the council as provided in Alternative II of §2.03.

(a) **Composition.** There shall be a city council composed of the mayor and [even-number] members. One council member shall be nominated and elected by the voters in each of [even-number] council districts. The mayor shall be elected in accordance with the provisions of §2.03.

(b) **Eligibility.** Only registered voters of the city shall be eligible to hold the office of council member or mayor.

(c) **Election and Terms.** The regular election of council members shall be held on the _____ of _____ in each odd- [even-] numbered year, in the manner provided by law. At the first election under this charter _____ council members shall be elected; council members from odd-numbered districts shall serve for terms of two years, and council members from even-numbered districts shall serve for terms of four years. Thereafter, all council members shall serve for terms of four years. The terms of council members shall begin the _____ day of _____ after their election.

NOTE: If staggered terms are not desired, use the following section.

[(c) **Election and Terms.** The regular election of council members shall be held on the _____ day of _____ every _____ years beginning in _____. The terms of council members shall be _____ years beginning the _____ day of _____ after their election.]

Alternative V
(Proportional Representation)

(a) **Composition and Term.** There shall be a city council of [odd-number] members elected by the registered voters of the city at large for a term of _____ years.

(b) **Eligibility.** Only registered voters of the city shall be eligible to hold the office of council member.

(c) **Election.** The regular election of council members shall be held on the _____ of _____ in each odd- [even-] numbered year. The Council shall be elected by proportional representation by the method of the single transferable vote.

Section 2.03. Mayor

Alternative I

At each regular election a mayor shall be elected for a term of _____ [the same term as other council members] years. The mayor shall be a member of the city council and shall preside at meetings of the council, represent the city in intergovernmental relationships, appoint with the advice and consent of the council the members of citizen advisory boards and commissions, present an annual state of the city message, and perform other duties specified by the council. The mayor shall be recognized as head of the city government for all ceremonial purposes and by the governor for purposes of military law but shall have no administrative duties. The council shall elect from among its members a deputy mayor who shall act as mayor during the absence or disability of the mayor and, if a vacancy occurs, shall become mayor for the remainder of the unexpired term.

Alternative II

The city council shall elect from among its members officers of the city who shall have the titles of mayor and deputy mayor, each of whom shall serve at the pleasure of the council. The mayor shall preside at meetings of the council, represent the city in intergovernmental relationships, appoint with the advice and consent of the council the members of citizen advisory boards and commissions, present an annual state of the city message, and other duties specified by the council. The mayor shall be recognized as head of the city government for all ceremonial purposes and by the governor for purposes of military law but shall have no administrative duties. The deputy mayor shall act as mayor during the absence or disability of the mayor.

Section 2.04. Compensation; Expenses.

The city council may determine the annual salary of the mayor and council members by ordinance, but no ordinance increasing such salary shall become effective until the date of commencement of the terms of council members elected at the next regular election. The mayor and council members shall receive their actual and necessary expenses incurred in the performance of their duties of office.

Section 2.05. Prohibitions.

(a) **Holding Other Office.** Except where authorized by law, no council member shall hold any other elected public office during the term for which the member was elected to the council. No council member shall hold any other city office or employment during the terms for which the member was elected to the council. No former council member shall hold any compensated appointive office or employment with the city until one year after the expiration of the term for which the member was elected to the council. Nothing in this section shall be construed to prohibit the council from selecting any current or former council member to represent the city on the governing board of any regional or other intergovernmental agency.

(b) **Appointments and Removals.** Neither the city council nor any of its members shall in any manner control or demand the appointment or removal of any city administrative officer or employee whom the city manager or any subordinate of the city manager is empowered to appoint, but the council may express its views and fully and freely discuss with the city manager anything pertaining to appointment and removal of such officers and employees.

(c) **Interference with Administration.** Except for the purpose of inquiries and investigations under §2.09, the council or its members shall deal with city officers and employees who are subject to the direction and supervision of the city manager solely through the city manager, and neither the council nor its members shall give orders to any such officer or employee, either publicly or privately.

Section 2.06. Vacancies; Forfeiture of Office; Filling of Vacancies.
(a) **Vacancies.** The office of a council member shall become vacant upon the member's death, resignation, removal from office or forfeiture of office in any manner authorized by law.

(b) **Forfeiture of Office.** A council member shall forfeit that office if the council member

(1) lacks at any time during the term of office for which elected any qualification for the office prescribed by this charter or by law,

(2) violates any express prohibition of this charter,

(3) is convicted of a crime involving moral turpitude, or

(4) fails to attend three consecutive regular meetings of the council without being excused by the council.

(c) **Filling of Vacancies.** A vacancy in the city council shall be filled for the remainder of the unexpired term, if any, at the next regular election following not less than 60 days upon the occurrence of the vacancy, but the council by a majority vote of all its remaining members shall appoint a qualified person to fill the vacancy until the person elected to serve the remainder of the unexpired term takes office. If the council fails to do so within 30 days following the occurrence of the vacancy, the election authorities shall call a special election to fill the vacancy, to be held not sooner than 90 days and not later than 120 days following the occurrence of the vacancy, and to be otherwise governed by law. Notwithstanding the requirement in §2.11, if at any time the membership of the council is reduced to less than _____, the remaining members may by majority action appoint additional members to raise the membership to _____.

Section 2.07. Judge of Qualifications.
The city council shall be the judge of the election and qualifications of its members and of the grounds for forfeiture of their office. The council shall have the power to set additional standards of conduct for its members beyond those specified in the charter and may provide for such penalties as it deems appropriate, including forfeiture of office. In order to exercise these powers, the council shall have power to subpoena witnesses, administer oaths and require the production of evidence. A member charged with conduct constituting grounds for forfeiture of office shall be entitled to a public hearing on demand, and notice of such hearing shall be published in one or more newspapers of general circulation in the city at least one week in advance of the hearing. Decisions made by the council under this section shall be subject to judicial review.

Section 2.08. City Clerk.
The city council shall appoint an officer of the city who shall have the title of city clerk. The city clerk shall give notice of council meetings to its members and the public, keep the journal of its proceedings and perform such other duties as are assigned by this charter or by the council or by state law.

Section 2.09. Investigations.
The city council may make investigations into the affairs of the city and the conduct of any city department, office or agency and for this purpose may subpoena witnesses, administer oaths, take testimony and require the production of evidence. Failure or refusal to obey a lawful order issued in the exercise of these powers by the council shall be a misdemeanor punishable

by a fine of not more than $\_\_\_\_\_$, or by imprisonment for not more than
_____ or both.

Section 2.10. Independent Audit.
The city council shall provide for an independent annual audit of all city
accounts and may provide for more frequent audits as it deems necessary.
Such audits shall be made by a certified public accountant or firm of such
accountants who have no personal interest, direct or indirect, in the fiscal
affairs of the city government or any of its officers. The council may, without requiring competitive bids, designate such accountant or firm annually or for a period not exceeding three years, but the designation for any
particular fiscal year shall be made no later than 30 days after the beginning of such fiscal year. If the state makes such an audit, the council may
accept it as satisfying the requirements of this section.

Section 2.11. Procedure.
(a) **Meetings.** The council shall meet regularly at least once in every month
at such times and places as the council may prescribe by rule. Special meetings may be held on the call of the mayor or of _____ or more members
and, whenever practicable, upon no less than twelve hours notice to each
member. Except as allowed by state law, all meetings shall be public; however, the council may recess for the purpose of discussing in a closed or
executive session limited to its own membership any matter which would
tend to defame or prejudice the character or reputation of any person, if
the general subject matter for consideration is expressed in the motion
calling for such session and final action on such motion is not taken by
the council until the matter is placed on the agenda.

(b) **Rules and Journal.** The city council shall determine its own rules and
order of business and shall provide for keeping a journal of its proceedings. This journal shall be a public record.

(c) **Voting.** Voting, except on procedural motions, shall be by roll call and
the ayes and nays shall be recorded in the journal. _____ members of the
council shall constitute a quorum, but a smaller number may adjourn
from time to time and may compel the attendance of absent members in
the manner and subject to the penalties prescribed by the rules of the council. No action of the council, except as otherwise provided in the preceding sentence and in §2.06, shall be valid or binding unless adopted by the
affirmative vote of _____ or more members of the council.

Section 2.12. Action Requiring an Ordinance.
In addition to other acts required by law or by specific provision of this charter to be done by ordinance, those acts of the city council shall be by ordinance which:

(1) Adopt or amend an administrative code or establish, alter, or abolish any city department, office or agency;

(2) Provide for a fine or other penalty or establish a rule or regulation for violation of which a fine or other penalty is imposed;

(3) Levy taxes;

(4) Grant, renew or extend a franchise;

(5) Regulate the rate charged for its services by a public utility;

(6) Authorize the borrowing of money;

(7) Convey or lease or authorize the conveyance or lease of any lands of the city;

(8) Regulate land use and development; and

(9) Amend or repeal any ordinance previously adopted.

Acts other than those referred to in the preceding sentence may be done either by ordinance or by resolution.

Section 2.13. Ordinances in General.
(a) **Form.** Every proposed ordinance shall be introduced in writing and in the form required for final adoption. No ordinance shall contain more than one subject which shall be clearly expressed in its title. The enacting clause shall be "The city of _____ hereby ordains ...." Any ordinance which repeals or amends an existing ordinance or part of the city code shall set out in full the ordinance, sections or subsections to be repealed or amended, and shall indicate matters to be omitted by enclosing it in brackets or by strikeout type and shall indicate new matters by underscoring or by italics.

(b) **Procedure.** An ordinance may be introduced by any member at any regular or special meeting of the council. Upon introduction of any ordinance, the city clerk shall distribute a copy to each council member and to the city manager, shall file a reasonable number of copies in the office of the city clerk and such other public places as the council may designate, and shall publish the ordinance together with a notice setting out the time and place for a public hearing thereon and for its consideration by the council. The public hearing shall follow the publication by at least seven days, may be held separately or in connection with a regular or special council meeting and may be adjourned from time to time; all persons interested shall have an opportunity to be heard. After the hearing the council may adopt the ordinance with or without amendment or reject it, but if it is amended as to any matter of substance, the council may not adopt it until the ordinance or its amended sections have been subjected to all the procedures herein before required in the case of a newly introduced ordinance. As soon as practicable after adoption, the clerk shall have the ordinance and a notice of its adoption published and available at a reasonable price.

(c) **Effective Date.** Except as otherwise provided in this charter, every adopted ordinance shall become effective at the expiration of 30 days after adoption or at any later date specified therein.

(d) **"Publish" Defined.** As used in this section, the term "publish" means to print in one or more newspapers of general circulation in the city: (1) The ordinance or a brief summary thereof, and (2) the places where copies of it have been filed and the times when they are available for public inspection and purchase at a reasonable price.

Section 2.14. Emergency Ordinances.
To meet a public emergency affecting life, health, property or the public peace, the city council may adopt one or more emergency ordinances, but such ordinances may not levy taxes, grant, renew or extend a franchise, regulate the rate charged by any public utility for its services or authorize the borrowing of money except as provided in §5.07(b). An emergency ordinance shall be introduced in the form and manner prescribed for ordinances generally, except that it shall be plainly designated as an emergency ordinance and shall contain, after the enacting clause, a declaration stating that an emergency exists and describing it in clear and specific terms. An emergency ordinance may be adopted with or without amendment or rejected at the meeting at which it is introduced, but the affirmative vote of at least _____ members shall be required for adoption. After its adoption the ordinance shall be published and printed as prescribed for other adopted ordinances. It shall become effective upon adoption or at such

later time as it may specify. Every emergency ordinance except one made pursuant to §5.07(b) shall automatically stand repealed as of the 61st day following the date on which it was adopted, but this shall not prevent re-enactment of the ordinance in the manner specified in this section if the emergency still exists. An emergency ordinance may also be repealed by adoption of a repealing ordinance in the same manner specified in this section for adoption of emergency ordinances.

Section 2.15. Codes of Technical Regulations.

The city council may adopt any standard code of technical regulations by reference thereto in an adopting ordinance. The procedure and requirements governing such an adopting ordinance shall be as prescribed for ordinances generally except that:

(1) The requirements of §2.13 for distribution and filing of copies of the ordinance shall be construed to include copies of the code of technical regulations as well as of the adopting ordinance, and

(2) A copy of each adopted code of technical regulations as well as of the adopting ordinance shall be authenticated and recorded by the city clerk pursuant to §2.16(a).

Copies of any adopted code of technical regulations shall be made available by the city clerk for distribution or for purchase at a reasonable price.

Section 2.16. Authentication and Recording; Codification; Printing.

(a) **Authentication and Recording.** The city clerk shall authenticate by signing and shall record in full in a properly indexed book kept for the purpose all ordinances and resolutions adopted by the city council.

(b) **Codification.** Within three years after adoption of this charter and at least every ten years thereafter, the city council shall provide for the preparation of a general codification of all city ordinances and resolutions having the force and effect of law. The general codification shall be adopted by the council by ordinance and shall be published promptly in bound or loose-leaf form, together with this charter and any amendments thereto, pertinent provisions of the constitution and other laws of the state of _____, and such codes of technical regulations and other rules and regulations as the council may specify. This compilation shall be known and cited officially as the _____ city code. Copies of the code shall be furnished to city officers, placed in libraries and public offices for free public reference and made available for purchase by the public at a reasonable price fixed by the council.

(c) **Printing of Ordinances and Resolutions.** The city council shall cause each ordinance and resolution having the force and effect of law and each amendment to this charter to be printed promptly following its adoption, and the printed ordinances, resolutions and charter amendments shall be distributed or sold to the public at reasonable prices as fixed by the council. Following publication of the first _____ City Code and at all times thereafter, the ordinances, resolutions and charter amendments shall be printed in substantially the same style as the code currently in effect and shall be suitable in form for integration therein. The council shall make such further arrangements as it deems desirable with respect to reproduction and distribution of any current changes in or additions to the provisions of the constitution and other laws of the state of _____, or the codes of technical regulations and other rules and regulations included in the code.

Article III
CITY MANAGER

Section 3.01. Appointment; Qualifications; Compensation.

The city council by a majority vote of its total membership shall appoint a city manager for an indefinite term and fix the manager's compensation. The city manager shall be appointed solely on the basis of executive and administrative qualifications. The manager need not be a resident of the city or state at the time of appointment but may reside outside the city while in office only with the approval of the council.

Section 3.02. Removal.

The city manager may be suspended by a resolution approved by the majority of the total membership of the city council which shall set forth the reasons for suspension and proposed removal. A copy of such resolution shall be served immediately upon the city manager. The city manager shall have fifteen days in which to reply thereto in writing, and upon request, shall be afforded a public hearing, which shall occur not earlier than ten days nor later than fifteen days after such hearing is requested. After the public hearing, if one be requested, and after full consideration, the city council by a majority vote of its total membership may adopt a final resolution of removal. The city manager shall continue to receive full salary until the effective date of a final resolution of removal.

Section 3.03. Acting City Manager.

By letter filed with the city clerk, the city manager shall designate a city officer or employee to exercise the powers and perform the duties of city manager during the manager's temporary absence or disability. The city council may revoke such designation at any time and appoint another officer of the city to serve until the city manager returns.

Section 3.04. Powers and Duties of the City Manager.
The city manager shall be the chief administrative officer of the city, responsible to the Council for the administration of all city affairs placed in the manager's charge by or under this charter. The city manager shall:

(1) Appoint and, when necessary for the good of the service, suspend or remove all city employees and appointive administrative officers provided for, by or under this charter, except as otherwise provided by law, this charter or personnel rules adopted pursuant to this charter. The city manager may authorize any administrative officer subject to the manager's direction and supervision to exercise these powers with respect to subordinates in that officer's department, office or agency;

(2) Direct and supervise the administration of all departments, offices and agencies of the city, except as otherwise provided by this charter or by law;

(3) Attend all city council meetings. The city manager shall have the right to take part in discussion but shall not vote;

(4) See that all laws, provisions of this charter and acts of the city council, subject to enforcement by the city manager or by officers subject to the manager's direction and supervision, are faithfully executed;

(5) Prepare and submit the annual budget and capital program to the city council;

(6) Submit to the city council and make available to the public a complete report on the finances and administrative activities of the city as of the end of each fiscal year;

(7) Make such other reports as the city council may require concerning the operations of city departments, offices and agencies subject to the city manager's direction and supervision;

(8) Keep the city council fully advised as to the financial condition and future needs of the city;

(9) Make recommendations to the city council concerning the affairs of the city;

(10) Provide staff support services for the mayor and council members; and

(11) Perform such other duties as are specified in this charter or may be required by the city council.

Article IV
DEPARTMENTS, OFFICES AND AGENCIES

Section 4.01. General Provisions.

(a) **Creation of Departments.** The city council may establish city departments, offices or agencies in addition to those created by this charter and may prescribe the functions of all departments, offices and agencies, except that no function assigned by this charter to a particular department, office or agency may be discontinued or, unless this charter specifically so provides, assigned to any other.

(b) **Direction by City Manager.** All departments, offices and agencies under the direction and supervision of the city manager shall be administered by an officer appointed by and subject to the direction and supervision of the manager. With the consent of council, the city manager may serve as the head of one or more such departments, offices or agencies or may appoint one person as the head of two or more of them.

Section 4.02. Personnel System.

(a) **Merit Principle.** All appointments and promotions of city officers and employees shall be made solely on the basis of merit and fitness demonstrated by a valid and reliable examination or other evidence of competence.

(b) **Merit System.** Consistent with all applicable federal and state laws the city council shall provide by ordinance for the establishment, regulation and maintenance of a merit system governing personnel policies necessary to effective administration of the employees of the city's departments, offices and agencies, including but not limited to classification and pay plans, examinations, force reduction, removals, working conditions, provisional and exempt appointments, in-service training, grievances and relationships with employee organizations.

Section 4.03. Legal Officer.

Alternative I

There shall be a legal officer of the city appointed by the city manager as provided in §4.01(b). The legal officer shall serve as chief legal adviser to the city council, the manager and all city departments, offices and agencies, shall represent the city in all legal proceedings and shall perform any other duties prescribed by state law, by this charter or by ordinance.

Alternative II

There shall be a legal officer of the city appointed by the city manager subject to confirmation by the city council. The legal officer shall serve as chief legal adviser to the council, the manager and all city departments, offices and agencies, shall represent the city in all legal proceedings and shall perform any other duties prescribed by state law, by this charter or by ordinance.

Alternative III

There shall be a legal officer of the city appointed by the city council. The legal officer shall serve as chief legal adviser to the council, the city manager and all city departments, offices and agencies, shall represent the city in all legal proceedings and shall perform any other duties prescribed by state law, by this charter or by ordinance.

Section 4.04. Planning.
Consistent with all applicable federal and state laws with respect to land use, development and environmental protection, the city council shall:

(1) Designate an agency or agencies to carry out the planning function and such decision-making responsibilities as may be specified by ordinance;

(2) Adopt a comprehensive plan and determine to what extent zoning and other land use control ordinances must be consistent with the plan; and

(3) Adopt development regulations, to be specified by ordinance, to implement the plan.

Article V
FINANCIAL PROCEDURES

Section 5.01. Fiscal Year.
The fiscal year of the city shall begin on the first day of _____ and end on the last day of _____.

Section 5.02. Submission of Budget and Budget Message.
On or before the _____ day of _____ of each year, the city manager shall submit to the city council a budget for the ensuing fiscal year and an accompanying message.

Section 5.03. Budget Message.
The city manager's message shall explain the budget both in fiscal terms and in terms of the work programs. It shall outline the proposed financial policies of the city for the ensuing fiscal year, describe the important features of the budget, indicate any major changes from the current year in financial policies, expenditures, and revenues together with the reasons for such changes, summarize the city's debt position and include such other material as the city manager deems desirable.

Section 5.04. Budget.
The budget shall provide a complete financial plan of all city funds and activities for the ensuing fiscal year and, except as required by law or this charter, shall be in such form as the city manager deems desirable or the city council may require. The budget shall begin with a clear general summary of its contents; shall show in detail all estimated income, indicating the proposed property tax levy, and all proposed expenditures, including debt service, for the ensuing fiscal year; and shall be so arranged as to show comparative figures for actual and estimated income and expenditures of the current fiscal year and actual income and expenditures of the preceding fiscal year. It shall indicate in separate sections:

(1) The proposed goals and objectives and expenditures for current operations during the ensuing fiscal year, detailed for each fund by organization unit, and program, purpose or activity, and the method of financing such expenditures;

(2) Proposed capital expenditures during the ensuing fiscal year, detailed for each fund by organization unit when practicable, and the proposed method of financing each such capital expenditure; and

(3) The anticipated income and expense and profit and loss for the ensuing year for each utility or other enterprise fund operated by the city.

For any fund, the total of proposed expenditures shall not exceed the total of estimated income plus carried forward fund balance, exclusive of reserves.

Section 5.05. City Council Action on Budget.
(a) **Notice and hearing.** The city council shall publish in one or more newspapers of general circulation in the city the general summary of the budget and a notice stating:

(1) The times and places where copies of the message and budget are available for inspection by the public, and

(2) The time and place, not less than two weeks after such publication, for a public hearing on the budget.

(b) **Amendment Before Adoption.** After the public hearing, the city council may adopt the budget with or without amendment. In amending the budget, it may add or increase programs or amounts and may delete or decrease any programs or amounts, except expenditures required by law or for debt service or for an estimated cash deficit, provided that no amendment to the budget shall increase the authorized expenditures to an amount greater than total estimated income.

(c) **Adoption.** The city council shall adopt the budget on or before the _____ day of the _____ month of the fiscal year currently ending. If it fails to adopt the budget by this date, the budget proposed by the city manager shall go into effect.

Section 5.06. Appropriation and Revenue Ordinances.
To implement the adopted budget, the city council shall adopt, prior to the beginning of the ensuing fiscal year:

(a) an appropriation ordinance making appropriations by department or major organizational unit and authorizing a single appropriation for each program or activity;

(b) a tax levy ordinance authorizing the property tax levy or levies and setting the tax rate or rates; and

(c) any other ordinances required to authorize new revenues or to amend the rates or other features of existing taxes or other revenue sources.

Section 5.07. Amendments after Adoption.
(a) **Supplemental Appropriations.** If during the fiscal year the city manager certifies that there are available for appropriation revenues in excess of those estimated in the budget, the city council by ordinance may make supplemental appropriations for the year up to the amount of such excess.

(b) **Emergency Appropriations.** To meet a public emergency affecting life, health, property or the public peace, the city council may make emergency appropriations. Such appropriations may be made by emergency ordinance in accordance with the provisions of §2.14. To the extent that there are no available unappropriated revenues or a sufficient fund balance to meet such appropriations, the council may by such emergency ordinance authorize the issuance of emergency notes, which may be renewed from time to time, but the emergency notes and renewals of any fiscal year shall be paid not later than the last day of the fiscal year next succeeding that in which the emergency appropriation was made.

(c) **Reduction of Appropriations.** If at any time during the fiscal year it appears probable to the city manager that the revenues or fund balances available will be insufficient to finance the expenditures for which appropriations have been authorized, the manager shall report to the city council without delay, indicating the estimated amount of the deficit, any remedial action taken by the manager and recommendations as to any other steps to be taken. The council shall then take such further action as it deems necessary to prevent or reduce any deficit and for that purpose it may by ordinance reduce one or more appropriations.

(d) **Transfer of Appropriations.** At any time during the fiscal year the city council may by resolution transfer part or all of the unencumbered appropriation balance from one department or major organizational unit to the appropriation for other departments or major organizational units. The manager may transfer part or all of any unencumbered appropriation balances among programs within a department or organizational unit and shall report such transfers to the council in writing in a timely manner.

(e) **Limitation; Effective Date.** No appropriation for debt service may be reduced or transferred, and no appropriation may be reduced below any amount required by law to be appropriated or by more than the amount of the unencumbered balance thereof. The supplemental and emergency appropriations and reduction or transfer of appropriations authorized by this section may be made effective immediately upon adoption.

Section 5.08. Lapse of Appropriations.

Every appropriation, except an appropriation for a capital expenditure, shall lapse at the close of the fiscal year to the extent that it has not been expended or encumbered. An appropriation for a capital expenditure shall continue in force until expended, revised or repealed; the purpose of any such appropriation shall be deemed abandoned if three years pass without any disbursement from or encumbrance of the appropriation.

Section 5.09. Administration of the Budget.

The city council shall provide by ordinance the procedures for administering the budget.

Section 5.10. Overspending of Appropriations Prohibited.

No payment shall be made or obligation incurred against any allotment or appropriation except in accordance with appropriations duly made and unless the city manager or his designee first certifies that there is a sufficient unencumbered balance in such allotment or appropriation and that sufficient funds therefrom are or will be available to cover the claim or meet the obligation when it becomes due and payable. Any authorization of payment or incurring of obligation in violation of the provisions of this charter shall be void and any payment so made illegal. A violation of this provision shall be cause for removal of any officer who knowingly authorized or made such payment or incurred such obligation. Such officer may also be liable to the city for any amount so paid. Except where prohibited by law, however, nothing in this charter shall be construed to prevent the making or authorizing of payments or making of contracts for capital improvements to be financed wholly or partly by the issuance of bonds or to prevent the making of any contract or lease providing for payments beyond the end of the fiscal year, but only if such action is made or approved by ordinance.

Section 5.11. Capital Program.

(a) **Submission to City Council.** The city manager shall prepare and submit to the city council a five- [six-] year capital program no later than the final date for submission of the budget.

(b) **Contents.** The capital program shall include:

(1) A clear general summary of its contents;

(2) A list of all capital improvements and other capital expenditures which are proposed to be undertaken during the five [six] fiscal years next ensuing, with appropriate supporting information as to the necessity for each;

(3) Cost estimates and recommended time schedules for each improvement or other capital expenditure;

(4) Method of financing, upon which each capital expenditure is to be reliant; and

(5) The estimated annual cost of operating and maintaining the facilities to be constructed or acquired.

The above shall be revised and extended each year with regard to capital improvements still pending or in process of construction or acquisition.

Section 5.12. City Council Action on Capital Program.
(a) **Notice and Hearing.** The city council shall publish in one or more newspapers of general circulation in the city the general summary of the capital program and a notice stating:

(1) The times and places where copies of the capital program are available for inspection by the public, and

(2) The time and place, not less than two weeks after such publication, for a public hearing on the capital program.

(b) **Adoption.** The city council by resolution shall adopt the capital program with or without amendment after the public hearing and on or before the _____ day of the _____ month of the current fiscal year.

Section 5.13. Public Records.
Copies of the budget, capital program and appropriation and revenue ordinances shall be public records and shall be made available to the public at suitable places in the city.

Article VI
ELECTIONS

Section 6.01. City Elections.
(a) **Regular Elections.** The regular city election shall be held at the time established by state law.

(b) Registered Voter defined. All citizens legally registered under the constitution and laws of the state of _____ to vote in the city shall be registered voters of the city within the meaning of this charter.

(c) Conduct of Elections. The provisions of the general election laws of the state of _____ shall apply to elections held under this charter. All elections provided for by the charter shall be conducted by the election authorities established by law. Candidates shall run for office without party designation. For the conduct of city elections, for the prevention of fraud in such elections and for the recount of ballots in cases of doubt or fraud, the city council shall adopt ordinances consistent with law and this charter, and the election authorities may adopt further regulations consistent with law and this charter and the ordinances of the council. Such ordinances and regulations pertaining to elections shall be publicized in the manner of city ordinances generally.

Section 6.02. Council Districts; Adjustment of Districts. (for use with Alternatives II, III and IV of §2.02)
(a) Number of Districts. There shall be _____ city council districts.

(b) Districting Commission; Composition; Appointment; Terms; Vacancies; Compensation.

   (1) There shall be a districting commission consisting of five members. No more than two commission members may belong to the same political party. The city council shall appoint four members. These four members shall, with the affirmative vote of at least three, choose the fifth member who shall be chairman.

   (2) No member of the commission shall be employed by the city or hold any other elected or appointed position in the city.

   (3) The city council shall appoint the commission no later than one year and five months before the first general election of the city council after each federal decennial census. The commission's term shall end upon adoption of a districting plan, as set forth in §6.02(c).

   (4) In the event of a vacancy on the Commission by death, resignation or otherwise, the city council shall appoint a new member enrolled in the same political party from which his or her predecessor was selected, to serve the balance of the term remaining.

(5) No member of the districting commission shall be removed from office by the city council except for cause and upon notice and hearing.

(6) The members of the commission shall serve without compensation except that each member shall be allowed actual and necessary expenses to be audited in the same manner as other city charges.

(7) The commission may hire or contract for necessary staff assistance and may require agencies of city government to provide technical assistance. The commission shall have a budget as provided by the city council.

(c) Powers and Duties of the Commission; Hearings, Submissions and Approval of Plan.

(1) Following each decennial census, the commission shall consult the city council and shall prepare a plan for dividing the city into districts for the election of council members. In preparing the plan, the commission shall be guided by the criteria set forth in §6.02(d). The report on the plan shall include a map and description of districts recommended.

(2) The commission shall hold one or more public hearings not less than one month before it submits the plan to the city council. The commission shall make its plan available to the public for inspection and comment not less than one month before its public hearing.

(3) The commission shall submit its plan to the city council not less than one year before the first general election of the city council after each decennial census.

(4) The plan shall be deemed adopted by the city council unless disapproved within three weeks by the vote of the majority of all members of the city council. If the city council fails to adopt the plan, it shall return the plan to the commission with its objections, and with the objections of individual members of the council.

(5) Upon rejection of its plan, the commission shall prepare a revised plan and shall submit such revised plan to the city council no later than nine months before the first general election of the city council after the decennial census. Such revised plan shall be deemed adopted by the city council unless disapproved within two weeks

by the vote of two-thirds of all of the members of the city council and unless, by a vote of two-thirds of all of its members, the city council votes to file a petition in the _____ Court, _____ County, for a determination that the plan fails to meet the requirements of this charter. The city council shall file its petition no later than ten days after its disapproval of the plan. Upon a final determination upon appeal, if any, that the plan meets the requirements of this charter, the plan shall be deemed adopted by the city council and the commission shall deliver the plan to the city clerk. The plan delivered to the city clerk shall include a map and description of the districts.

(6) If in any year population figures are not available at least one year and five months before the first general election following the decennial census, the city council may by local law shorten the time period provided for districting commission action in subsections (2), (3), (4) and (5) of this section.

(d) **Districting Plan; Criteria.** In preparation of its plan for dividing the city into districts for the election of council members, the commission shall apply the following criteria which, to the extent practicable, shall be applied and given priority in the order in which they are herein set forth.

(1) Districts shall be equal in population except where deviations from equality result from the application of the provisions hereinafter set forth, but no such deviation may exceed five percent of the average population for all city council districts according to the figures available from the most recent census.

(2) Districts shall consist of contiguous territory; but land areas separated by waterways shall not be included in the same district unless said waterways are traversed by highway bridges, tunnels or regularly scheduled ferry services both termini of which are within the district, except that, population permitting, islands not connected to the mainland or to other islands by bridge, tunnel or regular ferry services shall be included in the same district as the nearest land area within the city and, where such subdivisions exist, within the same ward or equivalent subdivisions described in subdivision (5), below.

(3) No city block shall be divided in the formation of districts.

(4) In cities whose territory encompasses more than one county or portions of more than one county, the number of districts which
include territory in more than one county shall be as small as possible.

(5) In the establishment of districts within cities whose territory is
divided into wards or equivalent subdivisions whose boundaries
have remained substantially unaltered for at least fifteen years, the
number of such wards or equivalent subdivisions whose territory
is divided among more than one district shall be as small as possible.

(6) Consistent with the foregoing provisions, the aggregate length of
all district boundaries shall be as short as possible.

(e) **Effect of Enactment.** The new city council districts and boundaries
as of the date of enactment shall supersede previous council districts and
boundaries for all purposes of the next regular city election, including
nominations. The new districts and boundaries shall supersede previous
districts and boundaries for all other purposes as of the date on which all
council members elected at that regular city election take office.

[**Section 6.03. Initiative and Referendum.**
The powers of initiative and referendum are hereby reserved to the electors of the city. The provisions of the election law of the state of _____, as
they currently exist or may hereafter be amended or superseded, shall govern the exercise of the powers of initiative and referendum under this charter.]
NOTE: Section 6.03 is in brackets because not all states provide for the
initiative and referendum and it is possible that not all cities within the
states that do provide for it will choose to include the option in their
charters.

Article VII
GENERAL PROVISIONS

Section 7.01. Conflicts of Interest; Board of Ethics.
(a) **Conflicts of Interest.** The use of public office for private gain is prohibited. The city council shall implement this prohibition by ordinance. Regulations to this end shall include but not be limited to: acting in an official
capacity on matters in which the official has a private financial interest

clearly separate from that of the general public; the acceptance of gifts and other things of value; acting in a private capacity on matters dealt with as a public official, the use of confidential information; and appearances by city officials before other city agencies on behalf of private interests. This ordinance shall provide for reasonable public disclosure of finances by officials with major decision-making authority over monetary expenditures and contractual matters and, insofar as permissible under state law, shall provide for fines and imprisonment for violations.

(b) **Board of Ethics.** The city council shall, by ordinance, establish an independent board of ethics to administer and enforce the conflict of interest and financial disclosure ordinances. No member of the board may hold elective or appointed office under the city or any other government or hold any political party office. Insofar as possible under state law, the city council shall authorize the board to issue binding advisory opinions, conduct investigations on its own initiative and on referral or complaint, refer cases for prosecution, impose administrative fines, and to hire independent counsel. The city council shall appropriate sufficient funds to the board of ethics to enable it to perform the duties assigned to it.

Section 7.02. Prohibitions.
(a) **Activities Prohibited.**

(1) No person shall be appointed to or removed from, or in any way favored or discriminated against with respect to any city position or appointive city administrative office because of race, gender, age, handicap, religion, country of origin or political affiliation.

(2) No person shall willfully make any false statement, certificate, mark, rating or report in regard to any test, certification or appointment under the provisions of this charter or the rules and regulations made thereunder, or in any manner commit or attempt to commit any fraud preventing the impartial execution of such provisions, rules and regulations.

(3) No person who seeks appointment or promotion with respect to any city position or appointive city administrative office shall directly or indirectly give, render or pay any money, service or other valuable thing to any person for or in connection with his or her test, appointment, proposed appointment, promotion or proposed promotion.

(4) No person shall knowingly or willfully solicit or assist in soliciting any assessment, subscription or contribution for any political party or political purpose to be used in conjunction with any city election from any city employee.

(5) No city employee shall knowingly or willfully make, solicit or receive any contribution to the campaign funds of any political party or committee to be used in a city election or to campaign funds to be used in support of or opposition to any candidate for election to city office or city ballot issue. Further, no city employee shall knowingly or willfully participate in any aspect of any political campaign on behalf of or opposition to any candidate for city office. This section shall not be construed to limit any person's right to exercise rights as a citizen to express opinions or to cast a vote nor shall it be construed to prohibit any person from active participation in political campaigns at any other level of government.

(b) Penalties. Any person convicted of a violation of this section shall be ineligible for a period of five years following such conviction to hold any city office or position and, if an officer or employee of the city, shall immediately forfeit his or her office or position. The city council shall establish by ordinance such further penalties as it may deem appropriate.

Article VIII
CHARTER AMENDMENT

Section 8.01. Proposal of Amendment.
Amendments to this charter may be framed and proposed:

(a) In the manner provided by law, or

(b) By ordinance of the city council containing the full text of the proposed amendment and effective upon adoption, or

(c) By report of a charter commission created by ordinance, or

(d) By the voters of the city.

When any five qualified voters initiate proceedings to amend the charter by filing with the city clerk an affidavit stating they will constitute the petitioners' committee and be responsible for circulating the petition and filing it in proper form, stating their names and addresses and specifying the address to which all notices to the committee are to be sent, and setting out in full the proposed charter amendment. Promptly after the affidavit of the petitioners' committee is filed the clerk shall issue the appropriate petition blanks to the petitioners' committee. The petitions shall contain or have attached thereto throughout their circulation the full text of the proposed charter amendment and must be signed by registered voters of the city in the number of at least twenty percent of the total number of registered voters at the last regular city election. The petitioners' committee may withdraw the petition at any time before the fifteenth day immediately preceding the day scheduled for the city vote on the amendment.

Section 8.02. Election.
Upon delivery to the city election authorities of the report of a charter commission or delivery by the city clerk of an adopted ordinance proposing an amendment pursuant to §8.01(b) or a petition finally determined sufficient proposing an amendment pursuant to §8.01(d), the election authorities shall submit the proposed amendment to the voters of the city at an election. Such election shall be announced by a notice containing the complete text of the proposed amendment and published in one or more newspapers of general circulation in the city at least 30 days prior to the date of the election. If the amendment is proposed by petition, the amendment may be withdrawn at any time prior to the fifteenth day preceding the day scheduled for the election by filing with the city clerk a request for withdrawal signed by at least four members of the petitioners' committee. The election shall be held not less than 60 and not more than 120 days after the adoption of the ordinance or report or the final determination of sufficiency of the petition proposing the amendment. If no regular election is to be held within that period, the city council shall provide for a special election on the proposed amendment; otherwise, the holding of a special election shall be as specified in the state election law.

Section 8.03. Adoption of Amendment.
If a majority of the registered voters of the city voting upon a proposed charter amendment vote in favor of it, the amendment shall become effective at the time fixed in the amendment or, if no time is therein fixed, 30 days after its adoption by the voters.

Article IX
TRANSITION/SEPARABILITY PROVISION

Section 9.01. Officers and Employees.
(a) **Rights and Privileges Preserved.** Nothing in this charter except as otherwise specifically provided shall affect or impair the rights or privileges of persons who are city officers or employees at the time of its adoption.

(b) **Continuance of Office or Employment.** Except as specifically provided by this charter, if at the time this charter takes full effect a city administrative officer or employee holds any office or position which is or can be abolished by or under this charter, he or she shall continue in such office or position until the taking effect of some specific provision under this charter directing that he or she vacate the office or position.

(c) **Personnel System.** An employee holding a city position at the time this charter takes full effect, who was serving in that same or a comparable position at the time of its adoption, shall not be subject to competitive tests as a condition of continuance in the same position but in all other respects shall be subject to the personnel system provided for in §4.02.

Section 9.02. Departments, Offices and Agencies.
(a) **Transfer of Powers.** If a city department, office or agency is abolished by this charter, the powers and duties given it by law shall be transferred to the city department, office or agency designated in this charter or, if the charter makes no provision, designated by the city council.

(b) **Property and Records.** All property, records and equipment of any department, office or agency existing when this charter is adopted shall be transferred to the department, office or agency assuming its powers and duties, but, in the event that the powers or duties are to be discontinued or divided between units or in the event that any conflict arises regarding a transfer, such property, records or equipment shall be transferred to one or more departments, offices or agencies designated by the city council in accordance with this charter.

Section 9.03. Pending Matters.
All rights, claims, actions, orders, contracts and legal administrative proceedings shall continue except as modified pursuant to the provisions of this charter and in each case shall be maintained, carried on or dealt with by the city department, office or agency appropriate under this charter.

Section 9.04. State and Municipal Laws.

(a) In General. All city ordinances, resolutions, orders and regulations which are in force when this charter becomes fully effective are repealed to the extent that they are inconsistent or interfere with the effective operation of this charter or of ordinances or resolutions adopted pursuant thereto. To the extent that the constitution and laws of the state of _____ permit, all laws relating to or affecting this city or its agencies, officers or employees which are in force when this charter becomes fully effective are superseded to the extent that they are inconsistent or interfere with the effective operation of this charter or of ordinances or resolutions adopted pursuant thereto.

(b) Specific Provisions. Without limitation of the general operation of subsection (a) or of the number or nature of the provisions to which it applies:

(1) The following laws and parts of laws generally affecting counties or city agencies, officers or employees are inapplicable to the city of _____ or its agencies, officers or employees: [enumeration]

(2) The following public local laws relating to the city of _____ are superseded: [enumeration]

(3) The following ordinances, resolutions, orders and regulations of _____ [former city governing body] are repealed: [enumeration]

Section 9.05. Schedule.

(a) First Election. At the time of its adoption, this charter shall be in effect to the extent necessary in order that the first election of members of the city council may be conducted in accordance with the provisions of this charter. The first election shall be held on the _____ of _____. The _____ [city officials to be designated] shall prepare and adopt temporary regulations applicable only to the first election and designed to insure its proper conduct and to prevent fraud and provide for recount of ballots in cases of doubt or fraud.

(b) Time of Taking Full Effect. The charter shall be in full effect for all purposes on and after the date and time of the first meeting of the newly elected city council provided in §9.05(c).

(c) First Council Meeting. On the _____ of _____ following the first election of city council members under this charter, the newly elected members of the council shall meet at _____ [time] at _____ [place]:

(1) For the purpose of electing the [mayor and] deputy mayor, appointing or considering the appointment of a city manager or acting city manager, and choosing, if it so desires, one of its members to act as temporary clerk pending appointment of a city clerk pursuant to §2.08; and

    Note: Omit bracketed words if Section 2.03, Alternative I is used.

(2) For the purpose of adopting ordinances and resolutions necessary to effect the transition of government under this charter and to maintain effective city government during that transition.

(d) **Temporary Ordinances.** In adopting ordinances as provided in §9.05(c), the city council shall follow the procedures prescribed in Article II, except that at its first meeting or any meeting held within 60 days thereafter, the council may adopt temporary ordinances to deal with cases in which there is an urgent need for prompt action in connection with the transition of government and in which the delay incident to the appropriate ordinance procedure would probably cause serious hardship or impairment of effective city government. Every temporary ordinance shall be plainly labelled as such but shall be introduced in the form and manner prescribed for ordinances generally. A temporary ordinance may be considered and may be adopted with or without amendment or rejected at the meeting at which it is introduced. After adoption of a temporary ordinance, the council shall cause it to be printed and published as prescribed for other adopted ordinances. A temporary ordinance shall become effective upon adoption or at such later time preceding automatic repeal under this subsection as it may specify, and the referendum power shall not extend to any such ordinance. Every temporary ordinance, including any amendments made thereto after adoption, shall automatically stand repealed as of the 91st day following the date on which it was adopted, renewed or otherwise continued except by adoption in the manner prescribed in Article II for ordinances of the kind concerned.

(e) **Initial Expenses.** The initial expenses of the city council, including the expense of recruiting a city manager, shall be paid by the city on vouchers signed by the council chairman.

(f) **Initial Salary of Mayor and Council Members.** The chairman of the council shall receive an annual salary in the amount of $_____ and each other council member in the amount of $_____, until such amount is changed by the council in accordance with the provisions of this charter.

Section 9.06. Separability.

If any provision of this charter is held invalid, the other provisions of the charter shall not be affected thereby. If the application of the charter or any of its provisions to any person or circumstance is held invalid, the application of the charter and its provisions to other persons or circumstances shall not be affected thereby.

– – – –

Editor's Note: A complete copy of this document may be obtained from the National Civic League, 1445 Market Street, Suite 300, Denver, Colorado 80202-1717, telephone (303) 571-4343.

Notes

1. Jonathan Justin, Professional Management and Responsive Government 267, *National Civic Review*, National Municipal League, Inc., New York, New York, June 1978.
2. *Ibid.*
3. *Ibid.*
4. Charles R. Adrian, *Governing Urban America* 214, McGraw Hill Pub. Co., Inc., New York, New York, 1977.
5. *Ibid.*
6. *Ibid.*
7. *Ibid.*
8. International City Management Association, Facts on the Council-Manager Plan 1, International City Management Assn., Washington, D.C., Sept. 1982.
9. Stillman, Richard J., *The Rise of the City Manager* 6, 7, University of New Mexico Press, Albuquerque, New Mexico, 1974.
10. *Ibid.*, page 8.
11. Several early books on city managers include a discussion on the business values of the council-manager plan, for example: Harry A. Toulmin, *The City Manager*, D. Appleton & Co., New York, New York, 1915, and Robert Rightor, *The City Manager in Dayton*, National Municipal League, Inc., New York, New York, 1919.
12. Stillman, note 9 supra, at 8, 9.
13. For example, see Frank J. Goodnow, *Politics and Administration*, 16, Macmillan Co., New York, New York, 1900.
14. Stillman, note 9, supra, at 10, 11.
15. International City Management Association, Ordinance for Establishing Council-Manager Plan 2, 3, International City Management Association, Washington, D.C., undated.

16. William H. Hansell, "Evolution and Change Characterize Council-Manager Government," *Public Management*, Vol. 82, No. 8, August 2000, International City-County Management Association, Washington, D.C.

Bibliography

Adrian, *Governing Urban America*, McGraw Hill Pub. Co., New York, New York, 1977.

Banfield & Wilson, *City Politics*, Harvard University Press, Cambridge, Massachusetts, 1963.

Booth, *Council-Manager Government in Small Cities, Public Management*, International City Management Assn., Washington, D.C., November 1973.

Boynton, *The Council-Manager Plan: A Historical Perspective, Public Management*, International City Management Assn., Washington, D.C., October 1974.

Hansel, *Evolution and Change Characterize Council-Manager Government*, Public Management, International City-County Management Association, Washington, D.C., August 2000.

International City Management Association, *The Council-Manager Plan: Answers to Your Questions*, International City Management Assn., Washington, D.C., February 1980.

_____, *Citizens' Guide to Council-Manager Plan: An Annotated Bibliography*, International City Management Assn., Washington, D.C., 1975.

_____, *Facts on the Council-Manager Plan*, International City Management Assn., Washington, D.C., September 1982.

Justin, "Professional Management and Responsive Government," *National Civic Review*, National Municipal League, Inc., New York, New York, June 1978.

Kennedy, "Should Your Town Have a Professional Manager?," *The Massachusetts Selectman*, Vol. XXXVI, No. 1, Massachusetts Municipal Assn., Boston, Massachusetts, Winter 1977.

Mosher, *Democracy and the Public Service*, Oxford University Press, New York, New York, 1968.

Mardis & Heissel, *When the Manager Plan Comes to Town*, Nation's Cities, National League of Cities, Washington, D.C., May 1971.

National Municipal League, *Questions and Answers About the Council-Manager Plan*, National Municipal League, Inc., New York, New York, 1974.

Nolting, *The Mayor's Right Hand*, Nation's Cities, National League of Cities, Washington, D.C., May 1974.

Stene, *Selecting a Professional Administrator: A Guide for Municipal Councils*, International City Management Assn., Washington, D.C., 1972.

Stillman, *The Rise of the City Manager*, University of New Mexico Press, Albuquerque, New Mexico, 1974.

Waldo, *The Administrative State*, Ronald Press, New York, New York, 1948.

County Government

Victor S. DeSantis

County government in the United States has undergone tremendous change during the last century. In one of the most well-known early studies of county governments, H.S. Gilbertson depicted them, unfortunately, as the "dark continent[s]" of American politics.[1] The characterization stemmed from the rampant corruption and incompetence that was associated with the political machines and boss rule at the turn of the century. By mid-century however, Clyde Snider, a prominent scholar of county government, reported optimistically about the modernization of county government organizations and the expansion of the county role in the federalist state.[2] By the mid-twentieth century, counties were asked to take on more functional responsibility and were better equipped to handle their new role. The period since the mid-century assessment of the state of the county can also be seen as a continuation of more significant involvement from county government in the operation of American democracy. Indeed, many of the recommendations offered by Snider to enhance county government further, such as authority centralized in a chief administrative officer position and increased power to conduct county business, have been instituted.

Historically, one of the most remarkable features of county govern-

Originally published as "County Government: A Century of Change," Municipal Year Book 1989. Published by the International City/County Management Association, Washington, D.C. Reprinted with permission of the publisher.

ment has been its stability as an American institution. The number of county units reported in the 1987 Census of Governments stands at 3,042.[3] This number has changed little from the 1942 total of 3,051 and the 1962 figure of 3,043. When viewed beside the steady increase in the number of municipal and special district governments over the same time frame, the stability appears even more dramatic.

Roots of the American County System

The evolution of the American county can be traced back to its use in Britain as an administrative arm of the national government.[4] The tradition of county government was well ingrained in the lives of the British colonists as they began to settle in North America, though the role of the county differed slightly depending on the region of the country. Regardless of the different roles delegated to the county, it is not surprising that the county unit as a layer between town and state governments should become a permanent fixture in America from its inception.

During the early colonial days, towns and counties were the basic units of local government in New England. While the towns were at the heart of local decision making with the annual town meeting, counties were established to carry out a variety of functions not performed by the smaller towns. Counties were responsible for such functions as judicial, military, and fiscal administration. However, even in the early days of the nation, the county operated in the background of the town government and failed to achieve the same level of importance. This tradition has remained throughout the history of New England. In fact, Connecticut and Rhode Island function without the existence of counties as organized units of government. Thus, the impression of the county as the "lost child" of local government was visible quite early.

The counties of the middle colonies held a position somewhat more important than those in New England and grew to be more instrumental in the delivery of public services. While performing the same duties as their New England counterparts, the counties of the middle colonies also became involved in law enforcement, with the county sheriff a principal focal point. The more important status of these counties allowed them to further their functional responsibilities to include road construction and maintenance and many welfare programs for the poor. In New York and New Jersey, one supervisor with taxation duties was elected from each town or township. In addition this taxation supervisor served on the county board of supervisors (or board of chosen freeholders as they became known in New Jersey). This county board had control over many of the county administrative functions. This arrangement of county government became the most traditional form of county government and later evolved into what is now known as the commission form. As the population spread westward, this pattern of county government became widely adopted by Midwestern areas.

Quite different from the system of local government adopted in either New England or the Middle Atlantic states was the system established in Virginia by the early settlers of the Tidewater region. Since the county covers a much larger geographic area, it performed better as the basic unit of local government in this region. This was primarily a reflection of the predominantly agricultural society with its widely dispersed rural population. This made it necessary to establish the county government as the primary unit of local government in the delivery of public services with much more importance than the smaller units of municipal government.

The early models of county government that developed in the different regions of the original colonies set forth the basic patterns of county government still in existence. Many of the foundations set out in these early forms continue to affect the ongoing administration of American counties.

Evolution of Modern County Government

Like other units of local government, counties are essentially creatures of the state government and have only derivative powers. As such, they have often been limited in the amount of freedom to conduct their internal affairs. The ability of a county or municipality to bring about more autonomy or self-government is acquired through home-rule provisions. The primary argument behind such provisions stems from the feeling that the local government has a better understanding of local needs and traditions and is better suited to handle such requests.

Historically, the movement toward greater autonomy and home-rule authority has come much slower for counties than for cities in many states. This is not to suggest, however, that all states have moved at a constant pace. Today, the National Association of Counties (NACo) reports that 36 of the 48 states with county governments grant those units some form of home-rule authority, either in the form of home-rule charters or optional forms of government.[5] Of those 36 states, 23 offer counties the ability to adopt a home-rule charter, while the remaining 13 offer counties limited autonomy through limited home-rule provisions or optional forms of government.

Regardless of the form of government, the trend toward such legal grants of authority from the states reached a peak during the period between 1972 and 1974, when nine of these provisions were passed.[6] However, autonomy is a much more recent phenomenon in most counties. As recently as 1965, only 18 states granted counties the right to choose from among optional forms or charter government.

While the scope of authority granted under these provisions varies widely, the powers can be divided into the general areas of structure, functional responsibility, and fiscal administration.[7] In the structural area, home-rule authority gives counties the authority to have a position of appointed manager, or the position of elected executive, or both. It gives counties the ability to change the method of electing commissioners and the size of the legislative board. Additionally, it enables counties to move away from the tradition of electing many of the other county administrative officials and to fill these positions by appointment instead.

The ability to change the basic structural arrangements in counties is based on the idea that there is not one best way to organize the governmental machinery. The newer demands placed on counties require that there be some flexibility in their operation. As Florence Zeller points out, movement away from the traditional structure allows for greater professionalism and more centralization and accountability through the addition of a county manager or county executive.[8] The charges of lack of professionalism and accountability are those most often leveled against the commission form of county government still mandated in some states. Giving counties the authority to institute changes through home-rule charters or optional forms has greatly enhanced their ability to deal with the growing complexity of local government.

In the area of functional responsibility, granting home authority can allow counties to increase their level of efficiency in public service provision. The ability to exercise independence in choosing alternative approaches for delivering public services has enabled some counties to better manage their resources. In addition to outright city-county consolidation, the use of intergovernmental service arrangements has allowed counties and their cities to avoid the duplicated and uncoordinated efforts that confront many neighboring jurisdictions. As Joseph Zimmerman points out, in 1974 only ten states had the constitutional or legislative authority to transfer voluntarily functional responsibility among units of government.[9]

Several types of functional arrangements can be used in the delivery of public services. The first involves a complete transfer of functional responsibility from one governmental unit to another. This has become more popular as many cities, under circumstances of fiscal stress, began realizing that the larger county unit may be better prepared to handle certain services. The other alternatives are to provide for an intergovernmental service contract or a joint service agreement. Under a service contract one or more cities can enter into a voluntary contract with the county to provide any number of services. A joint agreement may be entered into by a city and county for the joint financing and implementation of a service. A 1983 study by ICMA and ACIR showed that a substantial number of counties were using all three of these approaches, and the trend has increased over the previous decade.[10] Regardless of the approach used, counties are now handling the provision of more services than ever before. Clearly, this new responsibility indicates the growing role of the county in the intergovernmental framework.

The last area of powers granted under home-rule authority relates to fiscal administration. The ability of counties to control their own finances and promote budgetary stability is greatly enhanced when the rules governing county debt and revenue raising are loosened by the state government. Historically, counties were not free to issue bonds and raise debt limits on their own authority. Counties were also limited in their ability to raise revenue through taxation. Although there are wide differences, grants of fiscal control that accompany home-rule provisions allow counties greater financial flexibility to operate in the changing society. The current revenue data for counties point out the increased use of approaches that were not available to many counties until the last 20 years.

The trend toward greater autonomy suggests that counties have improved their position vis-à-vis the states over the past several decades. Interestingly, however, the rush toward adoption of home-rule charters has not proceeded quickly. Few counties in states that allow full home-rule charter provisions have attempted to institute such new forms. While this may suggest that many counties have made better use of the states' optional forms without going the full route toward self-determination that a home-rule charter would bring, it may also indicate other obstacles faced by counties in establishing home rule. One of the major obstacles involves the nature of charters themselves, which call for local approval. Many counties in the pursuit of local self-governance have tried and failed to establish home-rule charters. As Tanis Salant notes, "It appears an easier task for states to pass relevant proposals than it is for individual counties to adopt charters."[11]

Legally, the home-rule movement for counties has come far in affording counties a more substantial degree of self-governance. This may be the most important ingredient in promoting county modernization. According to Alastair McArthur, the ability of counties to move beyond the constitutional requirements mandated by the states is an important provision if counties are to confront the many demographic and economic changes that continue to occur.[12]

The City-County Consolidation Movement

One of the areas of change in intergovernmental relations has been the use of city-county consolidations. While this approach received popular support during the 1960s and early 1970s, the practice dates back to 1805 with the consolidation of New Orleans and Orleans County. A number of other large city and county areas also took this step by the turn of the century. Among them were New York, Boston, Philadelphia, and San Francisco.

A city-county consolidation involves the merger of one or more municipalities with a county to form a metropolitan government performing the functions of both cities and counties. Such consolidations can be established through voter referendum or state legislative action. Along with the governmental unification comes a merger of the geographic boundaries of the consolidated area. The current number of city-county consolidations stands at 21.

While the first half of the twentieth century saw few consolidations, the move toward this approach began to pick up again in the early 1960s. Unfortunately, while interest in this alternative had picked up, political and social realities confronting many areas trying to consolidate made success hard to come by. Some states have made consolidation difficult through restrictive provisions in the state constitution and statutes.

The benefits of consolidating an area come mainly in the provision and delivery of public services and the advantages that accrue from the consolidation of functional responsibility. Specifically, some of the frequent arguments in favor of consolidation are that it promotes efficiency and coordination in the provision of services, reduces the amount of governmental fragmentation, provides for greater resources by combining those of both areas, and reduces the need to establish special district governments.[13]

An independent city is one that performs the functions of both the city and the county but operates independently of any county unit. Though this phenomenon is found primarily in Virginia, in which there are 41 independent cities, several others also exist: St. Louis, Missouri; Baltimore, Maryland; and Washington, D.C.

Virginia is a special circumstance because it allows incorporated communities the ability to seek state legislative approval for designation as an independent city when the city reaches 5,000 in population and meets the requirements of the law to become a city. Such cities, if granted the designation, operate independently of any county governmental unit.

Form of Government

While a variety of different arrangements exist for the organization and administration of American counties, there remain three basic forms of county government: commission, council-administrator, and council-elected executive. Historically, the commission, or plural executive, form of government has served as the most extensively used form of county government. It has only been because of the more recent home-rule movements and optional form passages that county government has begun to use the alternative forms.

In order to gain precise information about the use of different forms of county government, ICMA conducted a "County Form of Government Survey" during the summer and fall of 1988. The survey included questions related to form of government, the county legislature, the chief elected officer, and the election process. The results of that survey form the database for this chapter.

The Commission Form. The commission or plural executive form of government in counties is the oldest and most traditional organizational structure. It is characterized by a central governing board with members usually elected by district. Though a variety of names exist for this board, among the favorite are the board of commissioners or supervisors and the county court (sometimes known as the levying court). Most often, the board selects one of its members as the presiding officer. Members of the governing board may act as department heads. The governing boards share administrative and, to an extent, legislative functions with independently elected officials: the clerk, the treasurer, the sheriff, the assessor, the coroner, the recorder, etc. No single administrator oversees the county's operations. In some counties with the commission form, the structure includes an official (generally full-time), such as the county judge, who is independently elected at-large to be the presiding officer of the governing board. As noted previously, many disadvantages associated with the commission form stem from the usual lack of a chief administrator to provide more professionalism, executive leadership, and accountability.

Among those counties that responded to the survey, the highest percentage use the commission form of government (39.7 percent). This is a relationship between form of county government and both population and metro status. The smaller and more rural counties are those that most frequently choose to remain under the traditional commission form. There would also appear to be substantial variation among the geographic divisions in the use of the commission form.

The Council-Administrator Form. Interestingly, the survey results point to increased usage of the council-administrator form and the council-elected executive form. While these findings may be partly a result of biases in the survey response group, the overall trend toward these two forms cannot be masked. In the past few years, counties have made dramatic leaps in moving toward these alternative structural arrangements.[14] Indeed, as noted previously, the overall trend toward professional management in counties can be seen by the ever-increasing number of counties recognized by ICMA as providing for the manager form of government.

The council-administrator form of government for counties is similar to the council-manager form for cities. But three distinct variations are identifiable. In its strongest variation, the council-administrator form provides for an elected county board or council and an appointed administrator. The county board adopts ordinances and resolutions, adopts the budget, and sets policy. The administrator, appointed by the board, has responsibility for budget development and implementation, the hiring and firing of department heads, and recommending policy to the board. In some counties, where a weaker version of the council-administrator plan is in place, the administrator usually has less direct responsibility for overall county operations and less authority in hiring and firing, and may consult with the board on policy issues.

There is more widespread use of the council-administrator plan among the more populated counties. This may be a result of the need for more professional management on a continual basis to accompany the complexity of governing large counties. While over half of the counties use this plan in each of the population groups above 50,000, none of the population groups below 50,000 use it with more than a 44.9 percent frequency. Counties with suburban status use this form most often, followed by counties with central status. The geographic breakdown reveals quite a high degree of variation also, with the South Atlantic counties having the highest percentage (75.6 percent) and the West South Central counties having the lowest rate (16.4 percent). Admittedly there is some degree of correlation between these variables. For example, the counties of the West South Central region are also those in Texas and other states that have a larger percentage of smaller rural county governments. In addition, the 254 Texas counties are mandated by state law to operate under the traditional commission form of government.

Another variation of the council-administrator form used in some areas combines elements of the council-administrator plan and the commission form. Here, an assistant to the presiding officer may serve in the capacity of administrator. For example, in Michigan the auditor, or controller, appointed by the governing board to audit the county's finances, may serve as an administrator; in other states, the county clerk, who is by statute clerk to the governing board, may have some administrative responsibility.

The Council-Elected Executive Form. The third form of county government is the council-elected executive form. This system has two branches of government — legislative and executive — and more clearly resembles the strong mayor form of city government. Here the county council or board assumes responsibility for county policies, adopts the budget, and audits the financial performance of the county. The elected at-large executive is considered the chief elected official of the county and often has veto power, which can be overridden by the council. The executive prepares the budget, carries out the administration of the county operations, appoints department heads (usually with the consent of the council), and suggests policy to the governing board. In addition, this official carries out appropriations, ordinances, and resolutions passed by the board and generally acts as the chief spokesperson for the county. When the executive is considered the chief political spokesperson, the executive often delegates the administrative responsibility for the daily county operations to a chief administrator.

This form, along with the council-administrator form, has begun to receive more popular support over the past several decades. In 1977, only 142 counties or about five percent operated under this form of county government, and those that did use it were often the larger more-populated counties.[15] A total of 269 (22.1 percent) of the responding counties reported operating under this form. Additionally, some noteworthy variations appear when this figure is broken down by population, region, and metro status. The counties in the population group between 500,000 and 1,000,000 put this form to use most frequently, with a percentage of 45.8 percent. None of the population groups below 250,000 reported using this form at a rate any higher than 24.9 percent. Regardless of such differences, the fact remains that this form has received much greater usage over recent years and has helped to push counties forward in their quest toward modernization.

Among the responding counties, 37.7 percent indicated that the county had established the position of chief administrative officer. When broken down by population group, it becomes clear that the larger counties are those that use the chief administrative officer most frequently. Not surprisingly, these results are similar to those for the council-administrator form of government. The majority of the counties report that the position was established through state statutes that allowed for the optional form. As noted previously, few counties have chosen to use the home-rule charter as a route to alter their form of government. Indeed only 7.3 percent claims to have established the position through a charter adoption. Additionally, of those that did use the charter as a means of acquiring a CAO, the highest percentage (53.8 percent) came in the second largest population group.

The Elected Head of County Government

While the official title of the presiding officer in counties has long been a traditional title such as county judge, county supervisor, or county board president, this has begun to change. The movement toward independently elected executives has made the title of county executive much more prevalent. Though the terms of office for the top official vary somewhat, almost all serve terms of less than five years. The greatest percentage of terms (58 percent) are only one year in duration. This is mostly an artifact of the plural executive form of county government in which the county council selects the presiding officer from among its members. This selection process may be a council vote or some rotational scheme. The rise in the number of two- and four-year terms may be a result of the increased use of the council-executive form, which allows the popularly elected executive the pleasure of a longer term.

The most popular method of selecting the elected head of county government is from the commission or council membership. While 69.1 percent use this method, only 22.2 percent of presiding officers are elected directly by the voters for that position. Few counties use an alternative method such as the rotation of a commission member to select their presiding officer.

Though the powers of the elected head of the county government vary among jurisdictions, one indication is the ability of the elected head to veto measures passed by the county council. The data shows few (8.1 percent) of the elected heads of government can veto council-passed measures. The breakdown by population group indicates that larger counties grant this right with the greatest frequency indicating this may be a function of the form of government, particularly the elected executive.

The County Legislature

One of the traditional aspects of county commissions is the smaller size of most legislative boards. Close to three-quarters (63.6 percent) of the county boards have sizes that range from three to five members. Another 15.2 percent range in size from six to ten members. A small percentage of county boards (5.6 percent) have over 20 members. The ability to increase the size of the county board is one of the reforms associated with the home-rule movement. The tradition of small councils is one that was long mandated by state requirements.

As previously mentioned, the presiding officer or elected head of the county government is often a member of the county board or council. As the data reflects, 93 percent of the responding counties indicated that the elected head of the government is also a member of the county board. This high percentage suggests that even under the council-executive form, the elected head may serve on the council in some capacity.

The length of the term for commission members is broken down between those elected from at-large and ward systems. Under both methods of election, the majority of commission members are elected to serve four-year terms. For those elected from at-large systems, 82.9 percent of commission members have four years to serve, while 75.9 percent serve four-year terms under ward systems. While there are small percentages of two-, three-, and over six-year terms in the at-large systems, the only substantial percentage of respondents (21.5 percent) in the ward system are those using two-year terms.

Use of overlapping terms in legislative bodies is one way of providing stability and continuity in the legislative process. The data indicates 69.5 percent of the responding counties allow for the overlap of commission member terms. The breakdown by population group reveals little relationship between the size of the county and overlap of commission member terms. However, it is noticeable that the overlap mechanism is used most often in the smaller counties (those under 5,000 in population).

The results indicate that there is substantial variation in overlap between geographic divisions. While the Mid-Atlantic and East South Central divisions use overlapping terms the least frequently, the West North Central and Pacific Coast use overlap most frequently. Metro status does not seem to be relevant to the use of overlapping terms.

The type of election system used in counties was also examined. The highest percentage of counties (45.5 percent) that responded indicated the use of district elections. For many counties without home-rule authority, the district plan is required under state law. While 30.1 percent use a system that mixes the at-large and district plan, only 24.4 percent use the pure at-large system. The predominant use of district elections in counties may stem from the larger size and more diverse nature of counties. While some geographic variations exist, there seems to be little correlation between either population or metro status. Populations of under 2,500 report use of at-large systems at a rate of 51.2 percent, an amount that is 15.9 percentage points higher than the next highest frequency of 35.3 percent.

One of the political reforms instituted in an effort to break the control of party organizations in local government was the establishment of nonpartisan elections. But only 17.6 percent of the responding counties have opted to exclude party labels from the election ballot. Further analysis of the partisan election phenomenon reveals that for those counties that have partisan elections, over 60 percent allow for the presence of both national and local party labels on the ballot. These election trends are surprising in light of the more widespread use of both at-large and nonpartisan election systems at the city level. Possibly the political reform movement that occurred so profoundly at the city level has never been felt as great at the county level.

County Finances

While the effects of fiscal stress on local governments is now a well-known reality, the problem remains an important aspect of managerial decision making. The tough decisions that are made to keep expenditures in line with revenues while citizens beckon for increased service levels remain with city and county administrators. While most managers have discovered new tools for dealing with such macrobudgetary issues, the impact of eight years of "new federalism" has been quite dramatic. One of the most detrimental policy changes may have been the demise of general revenue-sharing funds. In addition, many local government administrators have found their options limited in the wake of citizen initiatives to curtail the use of property taxes. Such efforts to hold down property tax rates have forced local governments around the country to look for alternative sources of revenue.

One of the most widely accepted alternatives has become current charges, or user fees as they are known. Current charges accounted for nearly one-quarter (24.8 percent) of the total county revenues in 1985–1986. In contrast, current charges made up roughly 16 percent of the total county revenue as recently as 1976–1977. While the future promises continued growth in the use of current charges, increases in functional assignments to counties may spell even more widespread use of this mechanism. Current charges, though somewhat controversial, can work to offset the costs of both delivering the public service and determining the level of service demanded by the citizens. Without question, however, the popularity of current charges as a revenue mechanism should continue to increase in the future.

In spite of the policy shifts at the federal level, intergovernmental fiscal transfers remain the greatest single source of county revenues. In 1985–1986, such revenue accounted for slightly over 35 percent of the total revenue pool. The revenue data from 1976–1977 show that intergovernmental revenue accounted for roughly 44 percent of the total county revenue. These figures point to a much reduced role for the federal and state government in their fiscal assistance to county governments.

The 1988 presidential election may have bolstered the hope of many local governmental officials, however. Many of them are taking an aggressive role in determining their economic fate. Such groups as the National Association of Counties, the National League of Cities, and the U.S. Conference of Mayors joined forces to lobby many of the presidential and congressional candidates long before the election in the hopes of getting local government support higher on the list of priorities in the upcoming years.[16]

Another trend in county revenues is the decreased reliance on property taxes as a revenue source. Though property taxes accounted for 26.2 percent of total revenue in 1985–1986, this amount represents a decline since 1976–1977 when over 30 percent of total revenue was acquired through property taxes. Offsetting this decline, however, has been the increase in non-property tax revenue over the same time period. While such taxes accounted for a mere seven percent of total revenue in 1976–1977, they made up nine percent of total revenue by 1985–1986.

Examination of the data reveal that counties have responsibility for provision of a variety of public service functions. The top three expenditure areas for county government in 1985–1986 are health and hospitals, public welfare, and education, in that order. This trend has remained consistent since 1979–1980.[17] The greatest percentage of county expenditures (15.9 percent) goes toward the maintenance and operation of hospitals and implementation of various health programs. This percentage has increased since 1979–1980 when the health and hospital expenditures accounted for 15.6 percent. While 14.3 percent of county expenditures was devoted to public welfare programs in 1985–1986, this represented a decrease on a percentage basis from the 1979–1980 figure of 15.3 percent. This decrease indicates the overall trend that has been seen as county spending in the area of public welfare decreases. During the early 1970s, the percentage of direct expenditures toward public welfare was roughly 25 percent.

The 1985–1986 expenditures in education account for 13.8 percent of total expenditures, down from 15 percent in 1979–1980. Importantly, these aggregates do not reveal the variations among the different states in county expenditure patterns. County educational expenditures for example are relatively high in those states in which counties are responsible for the direct administration of that function.

In the aggregate, county expenditures have increased dramatically during the 1980s. While counties spent over $56 billion in 1979–1980, the total expenditure increased to over $92 billion for 1985–1986. This represents an increase of 65.3 percent over the six-year period. However, revenues have increased at a slightly higher rate. While the total revenue amount in 1985–1986 was over $96 billion, in 1979–1980, the total revenue was just over $56 billion. The percentage increase in revenues between those time periods was 72.6 percent.

The date for the start of new fiscal years and the settling of the various revenue and expenditure reports required in modern government also shows some variation. While the highest percentage of counties (45.9 percent) opts for 1 January as the start of the new fiscal year, a large percentage also relies on the mid-year date of 1 July as a start of the fiscal cycle. Interestingly, only a small percentage of counties (11.2 percent) coordinates its fiscal cycle with the federal government's.

Conclusion

If counties were in a period of flux at the time of Snider's mid-century review, the same can be said of today's county government. The county government has grown in importance and plays an increasingly integral role in the intergovernmental framework. This can be seen most emphatically in the amount of service responsibility that has been granted to the county. While providing more services, they have also found new approaches to enhance their revenue base to cover the costs of delivering these services. Additionally, and most importantly, counties have been given more discretion in the organization and structure of their government through grants of home-rule charters and optional forms. These factors add up to a county government that is more professional, more flexible, and better equipped to handle the complexities that confront local governments in today's political and social environment. While much more remains to be accomplished at the county level, they clearly are an integral part of American politics.

Methodology

The data used in this survey were collected through ICMA's 1988 County Form of Government survey. The survey was mailed to county clerks in 3,044 counties in the United States. Counties not responding to the first request were sent a second survey. A total of 1,295 counties (42.5 percent) responded to the survey.

– – – –

Editor's Note: Professional management continues to grow among county governments in the United States. Between 1986 and 2000, the number of professionally-managed counties in the country grew from 650 to 1,151, by over 77%.

Like the council-manager form of organization in municipal governments, the number of county governments with a professional administrator has increased dramatically over the past decade. Table 2-1 documents the trend for county governments in the use of professional management for the effective governance of America's county governments.

The reader should keep in mind that this form of county government structure most reflects the will of those voters living within a county government's jurisdiction. County government residents, like municipal citizens, favor this type of high-trust government because it offers a politically neutral administration, and the separation of policy-making from day-to-day administration of the county government.

Table 2-1
Professional Management Continues to
Grow Among U.S. Counties

CAO Status	2000	1999[1]	1994	1990	1986
With Chief Administrative Officer	1,151[1] (37.8%)	1,032[1] (33.8%)	705 (23.2%)	677 (22.2%)	650 (21.4%)
Without Chief Administrative Officer	1,897[1] (62.2%)	2,020[1] (66.2%)	2,338 (76.8%)	2,367 (77.8%)	2,393 (78.6%)
Total	3,048	3,052	3,043	3,044	3,043
Form of Government	2000	1999[2]	1994	1990	1986
Council-Administrator	371 (12.2%)	372[2] (12.2%)			
Council-Elected Executive	480 (15.7%)	481[2] (15.8%)			
Commission	2,197 (72.1%)	2,200[2] (72.0%)			
Total	3,048	3,052	3,043	3,044	3,043

1. Statistics were obtained by pulling the number of counties with CAO positions listed in ICMA's database. These data do not appear in the Cumulative Distribution of Counties published annually in ICMA's Municipal Year Book.
2. The first year in which ICMA published county form-of-government data using this break-down was 1999.

Source: The Municipal Year Books 1986–2000, published by the International City/County Management Association (ICMA), Washington, D.C.

MODEL COUNTY GOVERNMENT CHARTER
John Parr

Article I
POWERS OF THE COUNTY

Section 1.01. Powers of the County.

The county shall have all powers possible for a county to have under the constitution and laws of this state as fully and completely as though they were specifically enumerated in this charter.

Section 1.02. Construction.

The powers of the county under this charter shall be construed liberally in favor of the county, and the specific mention of particular powers in the charter shall not be construed as limiting in any way the general power granted in this article.

Section 1.03. Intergovernmental Relations.

The county may exercise any of its powers or perform any of its functions and may participate in the financing thereof, jointly or in cooperation, by contract or otherwise, with any one or more states or any state civil division or agency, or the United States or any of its agencies.

Article II
COUNTY COUNCIL

Section 2.01. General Powers and Duties.

All powers of the county shall be vested in the county council, except as otherwise provided by law or this charter, and the council shall provide for the exercise thereof and for the performance of all duties and obligations imposed on the county by law.

Section 2.02. Composition, Eligibility, Election and Terms.

Alternative I: Election at Large

(a) **Composition.** There shall be a county council of [odd-number] members elected by the voters of the county at large.

(b) **Eligibility.** Only registered voters of the county shall be eligible to hold the office of council member.

(c) **Election and Terms.** The regular election of council members shall be held on the _____ of _____ in each odd- [even-] numbered year, in the manner provided by law. At the first election under this charter _____ council members shall be elected; the _____ [one-half plus one] candidates receiving the greatest number of votes shall serve for terms of four years, and the _____ [remainder of the council] candidates receiving the next greatest number of votes shall serve for terms of two years. Commencing at the next regular election and at all subsequent elections, all council members shall be elected for four-year terms. The terms of council members shall begin the _____ day of _____ after their election.

NOTE: If staggered terms are not desired, use the following section:

[(c) **Election and Terms.** The regular election of council members shall be held on the _____ day of _____ every _____years beginning in _____. The terms of council members shall be _____ years beginning the _____ day of _____ after their election.]

Alternative II: Election at Large with District Residency Requirement

(a) **Composition.** There shall be a county council of [odd-number] members; not more than one shall reside in each of the [odd-number] districts provided for in Article VI. All shall be nominated and elected by the voters of the county at large.

(b) **Eligibility.** Only registered voters of the county shall be eligible to hold the office of council member.

(c) **Election and Terms.** The regular election of council members shall be held on the _____ of _____ in each odd- [even-] numbered year, in the manner provided by law. At the first election under this charter _____ council members shall be elected; the _____ candidates receiving the greatest number of votes shall serve for terms of four years, and the _____ candidates receiving the next greatest number of votes shall serve for terms of two years. Thereafter, all council members shall be elected for four-year terms. The terms of council members shall begin the _____ day of _____ after their election.

NOTE: If staggered terms are not desired, use the following section.

[(c) **Election and Terms.** The regular election of council members shall be held on the _____ day of _____ every _____ years beginning in _____. The terms of council members shall be _____ years beginning the _____ day of _____ after their election.]

Alternative III: Mixed At-Large and Single-Member District System

(a) **Composition.** There shall be a county council of [odd-number] members. _____ shall be nominated and elected by the voters of the county at large, and _____ shall be nominated and elected by the voters of each of the _____ council districts, as provided in Article VI.

(b) **Eligibility.** Only registered voters of the county shall be eligible to hold the office of council member.

(c) **Election and Terms.** The terms of council members shall be _____ years beginning the _____ day of _____after their election.

Alternative IV: Single-Member District System

(a) **Composition.** There shall be a county council composed of [odd-number] members. One council member shall be nominated and elected by the voters in each of [odd-number] council districts, as provided in Article VI.

(b) **Eligibility.** Only registered voters of the county shall be eligible to hold the office of council member.

(c) **Election and Terms.** The regular election of council members shall be held on the _____ of _____ in each odd- [even-] numbered year, in the manner provided by law. At the first election under this charter _____ council members shall be elected; council members from odd-numbered districts shall serve for terms of two years, and council members from even-numbered districts shall serve for terms of four years. Thereafter, all council members shall serve for terms of four years. The terms of council members shall begin the _____ day of _____ after their election.

NOTE: **If staggered terms are not desired, use the following section.**

[(c) **Election and Terms.** The regular election of council members shall be held on the _____ day of _____ every _____ years beginning in _____. The terms of council members shall be _____ years beginning the _____ day of _____ after their election.]

Alternative V (Proportional Representation)

(a) **Composition and Terms.** There shall be a county council of [odd-number] members elected by the registered voters of the county at large for a term of _____ years.

(b) **Eligibility.** Only registered voters of the county shall be eligible to hold the office of council member.

(c) **Election.** The regular election of council members shall be held on the _____ of _____ in each odd- [even-] numbered year. The council shall be elected by proportional representation by the method of the single transferable vote.

Section 2.03 Chairman of the Council.

Alternative I

The county council shall elect from among its members officers of the county who shall have the titles of chairman and vice chairman of the council, each of whom shall serve at the pleasure of the council. The chairman shall preside at meetings of the council, represent the county in intergovernmental relationships, appoint with the advice and consent of the council the members of citizen advisory boards and commissions, present an annual state of the county message, and perform other duties specified by the council. The chairman shall be recognized as head of the county government for all ceremonial purposes and by the governor for purposes of military law but shall have no administrative duties. The vice chairman shall act as chairman during the absence or disability of the chairman.

Alternative II

NOTE: If Alternative II is used, Section 2.02(a) should be modified to read as follows: "There shall be a county council composed of the chairman of the council and [even-number] council members elected as provided in Section 2.02(c); the chairman shall be elected as provided in Section 2.03." Section 2.02(c) should be modified to provide for election of an even number of council members by whichever method is used.

At each regular election a Chairman of the Council shall be elected for a term of _____ [the same term as other council members] years. The chairman shall be a member of the county council and shall preside at meetings of the council, represent the county in intergovernmental relationships, appoint with the advice and consent of the council the members of citizen advisory boards and commissions, present an annual state of the county message, and perform other duties specified by the council. The chairman shall be recognized as head of the county government for all ceremonial purposes and by the governor for purposes of military law but shall have no administrative duties. The council shall elect from its members a vice chairman who shall act as chairman during the absence or disability of the chairman and, if a vacancy occurs, shall become chairman for the remainder of the unexpired term.

Section 2.04. Compensation; Expenses.

The county council may determine the annual salary of the council members by ordinance, but no ordinance increasing such salary shall become effective until the date of commencement of the terms of council members elected at the next regular election. The council members shall receive their actual and necessary expenses incurred in the performance of their duties of office.

Section 2.05. Prohibitions.

(a) **Holding Other Office.** Except where authorized by law, no council member shall hold any other elected public office during the term for which the member was elected to the council. No council member shall hold any other county office or employment during the terms for which the member was elected to the council. No former council member shall hold any compensated appointive office or employment with the county until one year after the expiration of the term for which the member was elected to the council. Nothing in this section shall be construed to prohibit the council from selecting any current or former council member to represent the county on the governing board of any regional or other intergovernmental agency.

(b) **Appointments and Removals.** Neither the county council nor any of its members shall in any manner control or demand the appointment or removal of any county administrative officer or employee whom the county manager or any subordinate of the county manager is empowered to appoint, but the council may express its views and fully and freely discuss with the county manager anything pertaining to appointment and removal of such officers and employees.

(c) **Interference with Administration.** Except for the purpose of inquiries and investigations under §2.09, the council or its members shall deal with county officers and employees who are subject to the direction and supervision of the county manager solely through the county manager, and neither the council nor its members shall give orders to any such officer or employee, either publicly or privately.

Section 2.06. Vacancies; Forfeiture of Office; Filling of Vacancies.
(a) **Vacancies.** The office of a council member shall become vacant upon the member's death, resignation, removal from office or forfeiture of office in any manner authorized by law.
(b) **Forfeiture of Office.** A council member shall forfeit that office if the council member
> (1) lacks at any time during the term of office for which elected any qualification for the office prescribed by this charter or by law,
> (2) violates any express prohibition of this charter,
> (3) is convicted of a crime involving moral turpitude, or
> (4) fails to attend three consecutive regular meetings of the council without being excused by the council.

(c) **Filling of Vacancies.** A vacancy in the county council shall be filled for the remainder of the unexpired term, if any, at the next regular election following not less than 60 days upon the occurrence of the vacancy, but the council by a majority vote of all its remaining members shall appoint a qualified person to fill the vacancy until the person elected to serve the remainder of the unexpired term takes office. If the council fails to do so within 30 days following the occurrence of the vacancy, the election authorities shall call a special election to fill the vacancy, to be held not sooner than 90 days and not later than 120 days following the occurrence of the vacancy, and to be otherwise governed by law. Notwithstanding the requirement in §2.11, if at any time the membership of the council is reduced to less than _____, the remaining members may by majority action appoint additional members to raise the membership to _____.

Section 2.07. Judge of Qualifications.
The county council shall be the judge of the election and qualifications of its members and of the grounds for forfeiture of their office. The council shall have the power to set additional standards of conduct for its members beyond those specified in the charter and may provide for such penalties as it deems appropriate, including forfeiture of office. In order to exercise these powers, the council shall have power to subpoena witnesses, administer oaths and require the production of evidence. A member charged with conduct constituting grounds for forfeiture of office shall

be entitled to a public hearing on demand, and notice of such hearing shall be published in one or more newspapers of general circulation in the county at least one week in advance of the hearing. Decisions made by the council under this section shall be subject to judicial review.

Section 2.08. County Clerk.

The county council shall appoint an officer of the county who shall have the title of county clerk. The county clerk shall give notice of council meetings to its members and the public, keep the journal of its proceedings and perform such other duties as are assigned by this charter or by the council or by state law.

Section 2.09. Investigations.

The county council may make investigations into the affairs of the county and the conduct of any county department, office or agency and for this purpose may subpoena witnesses, administer oaths, take testimony and require the production of evidence. Failure or refusal to obey a lawful order issued in the exercise of these powers by the council shall be a misdemeanor punishable by a fine of not more than $_____, or by imprisonment for not more than _____, or both.

Section 2.10. Independent Audit.

The county council shall provide for an independent annual audit of all county accounts and may provide for more frequent audits as it deems necessary. Such audits shall be made by a certified public accountant or firm of such accountants who have no personal interest, direct or indirect, in the fiscal affairs of the county government or any of its officers. The council may, without requiring competitive bids, designate such accountant or firm annually or for a period not exceeding three years, but the designation for any particular fiscal year shall be made no later than 30 days after the beginning of such fiscal year. If the state makes such an audit, the council may accept it as satisfying the requirements of this section.

Section 2.11. Procedure.

(a) **Meetings.** The council shall meet regularly at least once in every month at such times and places as the council may prescribe by rule. Special meetings may be held on the call of the chairman or of _____ or more members and, whenever practicable, upon no less than twelve hours notice to each member. Except as allowed by state law, all meetings shall be public; however, the council may recess for the purpose of discussing in a closed or executive session limited to its own membership any matter which would tend to defame or prejudice the character or reputation of any person, if the general subject matter for consideration is expressed in the motion calling for such session and final action on such motion is not taken by the council until the matter is placed on the agenda.

(b) **Rules and Journal.** The county council shall determine its own rules and order of business and shall provide for keeping a journal of its proceedings. This journal shall be a public record.

(c) **Voting.** Voting, except on procedural motions, shall be by roll call and the ayes and nays shall be recorded in the journal. _____ members of the council shall constitute a quorum, but a smaller number may adjourn from time to time and may compel the attendance of absent members in the manner and subject to the penalties prescribed by the rules of the council. No action of the council, except as otherwise provided in the preceding sentence and in §2.06, shall be valid or binding unless adopted by the affirmative vote of _____ or more members of the council.

Section 2.12. Action Requiring an Ordinance.

In addition to other acts required by law or by specific provision of this charter to be done by ordinance, those acts of the county council shall be by ordinance which:

(1) Adopt or amend an administrative code or establish, alter, or abolish any county department, office or agency;

(2) Provide for a fine or other penalty or establish a rule or regulation for violation of which a fine or other penalty is imposed;

(3) Levy taxes;

(4) Grant, renew or extend a franchise;

(5) Regulate the rate charged for its service by a public utility;

(6) Authorize the borrowing of money;

(7) Convey or lease or authorize the conveyance or lease of any lands of the county;

(8) Regulate land use and development; and

(9) Amend or repeal any ordinance previously adopted.

Acts other than those referred to in the preceding sentence may be done either by ordinance or by resolution.

Section 2.13. Ordinances in General.

(a) **Forum.** Every proposed ordinance shall be introduced in writing and in the form required for final adoption. No ordinance shall contain more than one subject which shall be clearly expressed in its title. The enacting clause shall be "The county of _____ hereby ordains ..." Any ordinance which repeals or amends an existing ordinance or part of the county code shall set out in full the ordinance, sections or subsections to be repealed or amended, and shall indicate matters to be omitted by enclosing it in brackets or by strikeout type and shall indicate new matters by underscoring or by italics.

(b) **Procedure.** An ordinance may be introduced by any member at any regular or special meeting of the council. Upon introduction of any ordinance, the county clerk shall distribute a copy to each council member and to the county manager, shall file a reasonable number of copies in the office of the county clerk and such other public places as the council may designate, and shall publish the ordinance together with a notice setting out the time and place for a public hearing thereon and for its consideration by the council. The public hearing shall follow the publication by at least seven days, may be held separately or in connection with a regular or special council meeting and may be adjourned from time to time; all persons interested shall have an opportunity to be heard. After the hearing the council may adopt the ordinance with or without amendment or reject it, but if it is amended as to any matter of substance, the council may not adopt it until the ordinance or its amended sections have been subjected to all the procedures herein before required in the case of a newly introduced ordinance. As soon as practicable after adoption, the clerk shall have the ordinance and a notice of its adoption published and available at a reasonable price.

(c) **Effective Date.** Except as otherwise provided in this charter, every adopted ordinance shall become effective at the expiration of 30 days after adoption or at any later date specified therein.

(d) **"Publish" Defined.** As used in this section, the term "publish" means to print in one or more newspapers of general circulation in the county: (1) The ordinance or a brief summary thereof, and (2) the places where copies of it have been filed and the times when they are available for public inspection and purchase at a reasonable price.

Section 2.14. Emergency Ordinances.

To meet a public emergency affecting life, health, property or the public peace, the county council may adopt one or more emergency ordinances, but such ordinances may not levy taxes, grant, renew or extend a franchise, regulate the rate charged by any public utility for its services or authorize the borrowing of money except as provided in §5.07(b). An emergency ordinance shall be introduced in the form and manner prescribed for ordinances generally, except that it shall be plainly designated as an emergency ordinance and shall contain, after the enacting clause, a declaration stating that an emergency exists and describing it in clear and specific terms. An emergency ordinance may be adopted with or without amendment or rejected at the meeting at which it is introduced, but the affirmative vote of at least _____ members shall be required for adoption. After its adoption the ordinance shall be published and printed as prescribed for other adopted ordinances. It shall become effective upon adoption or at such later time as it may specify. Every emergency ordinance except one made pursuant to §5.07(b) shall automatically stand repealed as of the 61st day following the date on which it was adopted, but this shall not prevent re-enactment of the ordinance in the manner specified in this section if the emergency still exists. An emergency ordinance may also be repealed by adoption of a repealing ordinance in the same manner specified in this section for adoption of emergency ordinances.

Section 2.15. Codes of Technical Regulations.

The county council may adopt any standard code of technical regulations by reference thereto in an adopting ordinance. The procedure and requirements governing such an adopting ordinance shall be as prescribed for ordinances generally except that:

(1) The requirements of §2.13 for distribution and filing of copies of the ordinance shall be construed to include copies of the code of technical regulations as well as of the adopting ordinance, and

(2) A copy of each adopted code of technical regulations as well as of the adopting ordinance shall be authenticated and recorded by the county clerk pursuant to §2.16(a).

Copies of any adopted code of technical regulations shall be made available by the county clerk for distribution or for purchase at a reasonable price.

Section 2.16. Authentication and Recording; Codification; Printing.

(a) **Authentication and Recording.** The county clerk shall authenticate by signing and shall record in full in a properly indexed book kept for the purpose all ordinances and resolutions adopted by the county council.

(b) **Codification.** Within three years after adoption of this charter and at least every ten years thereafter, the county council shall provide for the preparation of a general codification of all county ordinances and resolutions having the force and effect of law. The general codification shall be adopted by the council by ordinance and shall be published promptly in bound or loose-leaf form, together with this charter and any amendments thereto, pertinent provisions of the constitution and other laws of the state of _____, and such codes of technical regulations and other rules and regulations as the council may specify. This compilation shall be known and cited officially as the _____ county code. Copies of the code shall be furnished to county officers, placed in libraries and public offices for free public reference and made available for purchase by the public at a reasonable price fixed by the council.

(c) **Printing of Ordinances and Resolutions.** The county council shall cause each ordinance and resolution having the force and effect of law and each amendment to this charter to be printed promptly following its adoption, and the printed ordinances, resolutions and charter amendments shall be distributed or sold to the public at reasonable prices as fixed by the council. Following publication of the first _____ County Code and at all times thereafter, the ordinances, resolutions and charter amendments shall be printed in substantially the same style as the code currently in effect and shall be suitable in form for integration therein. The council shall make such further arrangements as it deems desirable with respect to reproduction and distribution of any current changes in or additions to the provisions of the constitution and other laws of the state of _____, or the codes of technical regulations and other rules and regulations included in the code.

Article III
COUNTY MANAGER

Section 3.01. Appointment; Qualifications; Compensation.

The county council by a majority vote of its total membership shall appoint a county manager for an indefinite term and fix the manager's compensation. The county manager shall be appointed solely on the basis of executive and administrative qualifications. The manager need not be a resident of the county or state at the time of appointment, but may reside outside the county while in office only with the approval of the council.

Section 3.02. Removal.

The county manager may be suspended by a resolution approved by the majority of the total membership of the county council which shall set forth the reasons for suspension and proposed removal. A copy of such resolution shall be served immediately upon the county manager. The county manager shall have fifteen days in which to reply thereto in writing, and upon request, shall be afforded a public hearing, which shall occur not earlier than ten days nor later than fifteen days after such hearing is requested. After the public hearing, if one is requested, and after full consideration, the county council by a majority vote of its total membership may adopt a final resolution of removal. The county manager shall continue to receive full salary until the effective date of a final resolution of removal.

Section 3.03. Acting County Manager.

By letter filed with the county clerk, the county manager shall designate a county officer or employee to exercise the powers and perform the duties of county manager during the manager's temporary absence or disability. The county council may revoke such designation at any time and appoint another officer of the county to serve until the county manager returns.

Section 3.04. Powers and Duties of the County Manager.

The county manager shall be the chief administrative officer of the county, responsible to the Council for the administration of all county affairs placed in the manager's charge by or under this charter. The county manager shall:

(1) Appoint and, when necessary for the good of the service, suspend or remove all county employees and appointive administrative officers provided for by or under this charter, except as otherwise provided by law, this charter or personnel rules adopted pursuant to this charter. The county manager may authorize any administrative officer subject to the manager's direction and supervision to exercise these powers with respect to subordinates in that officer's department, office or agency;

(2) Direct and supervise the administration of all departments, offices and agencies of the county, except as otherwise provided by this charter or by law;

(3) Attend all county council meetings. The county manager shall have the right to take part in discussion but shall not vote;

(4) See that all laws, provisions of this charter and acts of the county council, subject to enforcement by the county manager or by officers subject to the manager's direction and supervision, are faithfully executed;

(5) Prepare and submit the annual budget and capital program to the county council;

(6) Submit to the county council and make available to the public a complete report on the finances and administrative activities of the county as of the end of each fiscal year;

(7) Make such other reports as the county council may require concerning the operations of county departments, offices and agencies subject to the county manager's direction and supervision;

(8) Keep the county council fully advised as to the financial condition and future needs of the county;

(9) Make recommendations to the county council concerning the affairs of the county;

(10) Provide staff support services for the council members; and

(11) Perform such other duties as are specified in this charter or may be required by the county council.

Article IV
DEPARTMENTS, OFFICES AND AGENCIES

Section 4.01. General Provisions.

(a) **Creation of Departments.** The county council may establish county departments, offices or agencies in addition to those created by this charter and may prescribe the functions of all departments, offices and agencies, except that no function assigned by this charter to a particular department, office or agency may be discontinued or, unless this charter specifically so provides, assigned to any other.

(b) **Direction by County Manager.** All departments, offices and agencies under the direction and supervision of the county manager shall be administered by an officer appointed by and subject to the direction and supervision of the manager. With the consent of council, the county manager may serve as the head of one or more such departments, offices or agencies or may appoint one person as the head of two or more of them.

Section 4.02. Personnel System.

(a) **Merit Principle.**

All appointments and promotions of county officers and employees shall be made solely on the basis of merit and fitness demonstrated by a valid and reliable examination or other evidence of competence.

(b) **Merit System.** Consistent with all applicable federal and state laws the county council shall provide by ordinance for the establishment, regulation and maintenance of a merit system governing personnel policies necessary to effective administration of the employees of the county's departments, offices and agencies, including but not limited to classification and pay plans, examinations, force reduction, removals, working conditions, provisional and exempt appointments, in-service training, grievances and relationships with employee organizations.

Section 4.03. Legal Officer.
Alternative I
There shall be a legal officer of the county appointed by the county manager as provided in §4.01(b). The legal officer shall serve as chief legal adviser to the county council, the manager and all county departments, offices and agencies, shall represent the county in all legal proceedings and shall perform any other duties prescribed by state law, by this charter or by ordinance.

Alternative II
There shall be a legal officer of the county appointed by the county manager subject to confirmation by the county council. The legal officer shall serve as chief legal adviser to the council, the manager and all county departments, offices and agencies, shall represent the county in all legal proceedings and shall perform any other duties prescribed by state law, by this charter or by ordinance.

Alternative III
There shall be a legal officer of the county appointed by the county council. The legal officer shall serve as chief legal adviser to the council, the county manager and all county departments, offices and agencies, shall represent the county in all legal proceedings and shall perform any other duties prescribed by state law, by this charter or by ordinance.

Section 4.04. Planning.
Consistent with all applicable federal and state laws with respect to land use, development and environmental protection, the county council shall:

    (1) Designate an agency or agencies to carry out the planning function and such decision-making responsibilities as may be specified by ordinance;

    (2) Adopt a comprehensive plan and determine to what extent zoning and other land use control ordinances must be consistent with the plan; and

(3) Adopt development regulations, to be specified by ordinance, to implement the plan.

Article V
FINANCIAL PROCEDURES

Section 5.01. Fiscal Year.

The fiscal year of the county shall begin on the first day of _____ and end on the last day of _____.

Section 5.02. Submission of Budget and Budget Message.

On or before the _____ day of _____ of each year, the county manager shall submit to the county council a budget for the ensuing fiscal year and an accompanying message.

Section 5.03. Budget Message.

The county manager's message shall explain the budget both in fiscal terms and in terms of the work programs. It shall outline the proposed financial policies of the county for the ensuing fiscal year, describe the important features of the budget, indicate any major changes from the current year in financial policies, expenditures, and revenues together with the reasons for such changes, summarize the county's debt position and include such other material as the county manager deems desirable.

Section 5.04. Budget.

The budget shall provide a complete financial plan of all county funds and activities for the ensuing fiscal year and, except as required by law or this charter, shall be in such form as the county manager deems desirable or the county council may require. The budget shall begin with a clear general summary of its contents; shall show in detail all estimated income, indicating the proposed property tax levy, and all proposed expenditures, including debt service, for the ensuing fiscal year; and shall be so arranged as to show comparative figures for actual and estimated income and expenditures of the current fiscal year and actual income and expenditures of the preceding fiscal year. It shall indicate in separate sections:

    (1) The proposed goals and objectives and expenditures for current operations during the ensuing fiscal year, detailed for each fund by organization unit, and program, purpose or activity, and the method of financing such expenditures;

    (2) Proposed capital expenditures during the ensuing fiscal year, detailed for each fund by organization unit when practicable,

and the proposed method of financing each such capital expenditure; and

(3) The anticipated income and expense and profit and loss for the ensuing year for each utility or other enterprise fund operated by the county.

For any fund, the total of proposed expenditures shall not exceed the total of estimated income plus carried forward fund balance, exclusive of reserves.

Section 5.05. County Council Action on Budget.

(a) **Notice and Hearing.** The county council shall publish in one or more newspapers of general circulation in the county the general summary of the budget and a notice stating:

(1) The times and places where copies of the message and budget are available for inspection by the public, and

(2) The time and place, not less than two weeks after such publication, for a public hearing on the budget.

(b) **Amendment Before Adoption.** After the public hearing, the county council may adopt the budget with or without amendment. In amending the budget, it may add or increase programs or amounts and may delete or decrease any programs or amounts, except expenditures required by law or for debt service or for an estimated cash deficit, provided that no amendment to the budget shall increase the authorized expenditures to an amount greater than total estimated income.

(c) **Adoption.** The county council shall adopt the budget on or before the _____ day of the _____ month of the fiscal year currently ending. If it fails to adopt the budget by this date, the budget proposed by the county manager shall go into effect.

Section 5.06. Appropriation and Revenue Ordinances.

To implement the adopted budget, the county council shall adopt, prior to the beginning of the ensuing fiscal year:

(a) an appropriation ordinance making appropriations by department or major organizational unit and authorizing a single appropriation for each program or activity;

(b) a tax levy ordinance authorizing the property tax levy or levies and setting the tax rate or rates; and

(c) any other ordinances required to authorize new revenues or to amend the rates or other features of existing taxes or other revenue sources.

Section 5.07. Amendments after Adoption.

(a) **Supplemental Appropriations.** If during the fiscal year the county manager certifies that there are available for appropriation revenues in excess of those estimated in the budget, the county council by ordinance may make supplemental appropriations for the year up to the amount of such excess.

(b) **Emergency Appropriations.** To meet a public emergency affecting life, health, property or the public peace, the county council may make emergency appropriations. Such appropriations may be made by emergency ordinance in accordance with the provisions of §2.14. To the extent that there are no available unappropriated revenues or a sufficient fund balance to meet such appropriations, the council may by such emergency ordinance authorize the issuance of emergency notes, which may be renewed from time to time, but the emergency notes and renewals of any fiscal year shall be paid not later than the last day of the fiscal year next succeeding that in which the emergency appropriation was made.

(c) **Reduction of Appropriations.** If at any time during the fiscal year it appears probable to the county manager that the revenues or fund balances available will be insufficient to finance the expenditures for which appropriations have been authorized, the manager shall report to the county council without delay, indicating the estimated amount of the deficit, any remedial action taken by the manager and recommendations as to any other steps to be taken. The council shall then take such further action as it deems necessary to prevent or reduce any deficit and for that purpose it may by ordinance reduce one or more appropriations.

(d) **Transfer of Appropriations.** At any time during the fiscal year the county council may by resolution transfer part or all of the unencumbered appropriation balance from one department or major organizational unit to the appropriation for other departments or major organizational units. The manager may transfer part or all of any unencumbered appropriation balances among programs within a department or organizational unit and shall report such transfers to the council in writing in a timely manner.

(e) **Limitation; Effective Date.** No appropriation for debt service may be reduced or transferred, and no appropriation may be reduced below any amount required by law to be appropriated or by more than the amount of the unencumbered balance thereof. The supplemental and emergency appropriations and reduction or transfer of appropriations authorized by this section may be made effective immediately upon adoption.

Section 5.08. Lapse of Appropriations.

Every appropriation, except an appropriation for a capital expenditure, shall lapse at the close of the fiscal year to the extent that it has not been expended or encumbered. An appropriation for a capital expenditure shall continue in force until expended, revised or repealed; the purpose of any such appropriation shall be deemed abandoned if three years pass without any disbursement from or encumbrance of the appropriation.

Section 5.09 Administration of the Budget.

The county council shall provide by ordinance the procedures for administering the budget.

Section 5.10. Overspending of Appropriations Prohibited.

No payment shall be made or obligation incurred against any allotment or appropriation except in accordance with appropriations duly made and unless the county manager or the manager's designee first certifies that there is a sufficient unencumbered balance in such allotment or appropriation and that sufficient funds therefrom are or will be available to cover the claim or meet the obligation when it becomes due and payable. Any authorization of payment or incurring of obligation in violation of the provisions of this charter shall be void and any payment so made illegal. A violation of this provision shall be cause for removal of any officer who knowingly authorized or made such payment or incurred such obligation. Such officer may also be liable to the county for any amount so paid. Except where prohibited by law, however, nothing in this charter shall be construed to prevent the making or authorizing of payments or making of contracts for capital improvements to be financed wholly or partly by the issuance of bonds or to prevent the making of any contract or lease providing for payments beyond the end of the fiscal year, but only if such action is made or approved by ordinance.

Section 5.11. Capital Program.

(a) **Submission to County Council.** The county manager shall prepare and submit to the county council a five- [six-] year capital program no later than three months prior to the final date for submission of the budget.

(b) **Contents.** The capital program shall include:
   (1) A clear general summary of its contents;
   (2) A list of all capital improvements and other capital expenditures which are proposed to be undertaken during the five [six]

fiscal years next ensuing, with appropriate supporting information as to the necessity for each;
   (3) Cost estimates and recommended time schedules for each improvement or other capital expenditure;
   (4) Method of financing upon which each capital expenditure is to be reliant; and
   (5) The estimated annual cost of operating and maintaining the facilities to be constructed or acquired.

The above shall be revised and extended each year with regard to capital improvements still pending or in process of construction or acquisition.

Section 5.12. County Council Action on Capital Program.

(a) **Notice and Hearing.** The county council shall publish in one or more newspapers of general circulation in the county the general summary of the capital program and a notice stating:
   (1) The times and places where copies of the capital program are available for inspection by the public, and
   (2) The time and place, not less than two weeks after such publication, for a public hearing on the capital program.

(b) **Adoption.** The county council by resolution shall adopt the capital program with or without amendment after the public hearing and on or before the _____ day of the _____month of the current fiscal year.

Section 5.13. Public Records.

Copies of the budget, capital program and appropriation and revenue ordinances shall be public records and shall be made available to the public at suitable places in the county.

Article VI
COUNTY ELECTIONS

Section 6.01. County Elections.

(a) **Regular Elections.** The regular county election shall be held at the time established by state law.

(b) **Registered Voter Defined.** All citizens legally registered under the constitution and laws of the state of _____ to vote in the county shall be registered voters of the county within the meaning of this charter.

(c) **Conduct of Elections.** The provisions of the general election laws of the state of _____ shall apply to elections held under this charter. All elections provided for by the charter shall be conducted by the election authorities established by law. For the conduct of county elections, for the prevention of fraud in such elections and for the recount of ballots in cases of doubt or fraud, the county council shall adopt ordinances consistent with law and this charter, and the election authorities may adopt further regulations consistent with law and this charter and the ordinances of the council. Such ordinances and regulations pertaining to elections shall be publicized in the manner of county ordinances generally.

Section 6.02. Council Districts; Adjustment of Districts (for use with Alternatives II, III and IV of §2.01)

(a) **Number of Districts.** There shall be _____ county council districts.

(b) **Districting Commission; Composition; Appointment; Terms; Vacancies; Compensation.**

(1) There shall be a districting commission consisting of five members. No more than two commission members may belong to the same political party. The county council shall appoint four members. These four members shall, with the affirmative vote of at least three, choose the fifth member who shall be the chairman.

(2) No member of the commission shall be employed by the county or any political subdivision of the county, or hold any other elected or appointed position in the county or any political subdivision of the county.

(3) The county council shall appoint the commission no later than one year and five months before the first general election of the county council after each federal decennial census. The commission's term shall end upon adoption of a districting plan, as set forth in §6.02(c).

(4) In the event of a vacancy on the Commission by death, resignation or otherwise, the county council shall appoint a new member enrolled in the same political party from which his or her predecessor was selected, to serve the balance of the term remaining.

(5) No member of the districting commission shall be removed from office by the county council except for cause and upon notice and hearing.

(6) The members of the commission shall serve without compensation except that each member shall be allowed actual and

necessary expenses to be audited in the same manner as other county charges.

(7) The commission may hire or contract for necessary staff assistance and may require agencies of county government to provide technical assistance. The commission shall have a budget as provided by the county council.

(c) Powers and Duties of the Commission; Hearings, Submissions and Approval of Plan.

(1) Following each decennial census, the commission shall consult the county council and shall prepare a plan for dividing the county into districts for the election of council members. In preparing the plan, the commission shall be guided by the criteria set forth in §6.02(d). The report on the plan shall include a map and description of districts recommended.

(2) The commission shall hold one or more public hearings not less than one month before it submits the plan to the county council. The commission shall make its plan available to the public for inspection and comment not less than one month before its public hearing.

(3) The commission shall submit its plan to the county council not less than one year before the first general election of the county council after each decennial census.

(4) The plan shall be deemed adopted by the county council unless disapproved within three weeks by the vote of the majority of all members of the county council. If the county council fails to adopt the plan, it shall return the plan to the commission with its objections, and with the objections of individual members of the council.

(5) Upon rejection of its plan, the commission shall prepare a revised plan and shall submit such revised plan to the county council no later than nine months before the first general election of the county council after the decennial census. Such revised plan shall be deemed adopted by the county council unless disapproved within two weeks by the vote of two-thirds of all of the members of the county council and unless, by a vote of two-thirds of all of its members, the county council votes to file a petition in the _____ Court, _____ County, for a determination that the plan fails to meet the requirements of this charter. The county council shall file its petition no later than ten days after its disapproval of the plan. Upon a final

determination upon appeal, if any, that the plan meets the requirements of this charter, the plan shall be deemed adopted by the county council and the commission shall deliver the plan to the county clerk. The plan delivered to the county clerk shall include a map and description of the districts.

(6) If in any year population figures are not available at least one year and five months before the first general election following the decennial census, the county council may by ordinance shorten the time periods provided for districting commission action in subsections (2), (3), (4) and (5) of this section.

(d) **Districting Plan; Criteria.** In preparation of its plan for dividing the county into districts for the election of council members, the commission shall apply the following criteria which, to the extent practicable, shall be applied and given priority in the order in which they are herein set forth.

(1) Districts shall be equal in population except where deviations from equality result from the application of the provisions hereinafter set forth, but no such deviation may exceed five percent of the average population for all county council districts according to the figures available from the most recent census.

(2) Districts shall consist of contiguous territory; but land areas separated by waterways shall not be included in the same district unless said waterways are traversed by highway bridges, tunnels or regularly scheduled ferry services both termini of which are within the district, except that, population permitting, islands not connected to the mainland or to other islands by bridge, tunnel or regular ferry services shall be included in the same district as the nearest land area within the county and, where such subdivisions exist, within the same ward or equivalent subdivision as described in subsection (5), below.

(3) No city block shall be divided in the formation of districts.

(4) A municipality within a county shall be divided among as few districts as possible.

(5) In the establishment of districts within counties whose territory is divided into wards or equivalent subdivisions whose boundaries have remained substantially unaltered for at least fifteen years, the number of such wards or equivalent subdivisions whose territory is divided among more than one district shall be as small as possible.

(6) Consistent with the foregoing provisions, the aggregate length of all district boundaries shall be as short as possible.

(e) **Effect of Enactment.** The new county council districts and boundaries as of the date of enactment shall supersede previous council districts and boundaries for all purposes of the next regular county election, including nominations. The new districts and boundaries shall supersede previous districts and boundaries for all other purposes as of the date on which all council members elected at that regular county election take office.

[**Section 6.03. Initiative and Referendum.**

The powers of initiative and referendum are hereby reserved to the electors of the county. The provisions of the election law of the state of _____, as they currently exist or may hereafter be amended or superseded, shall govern the exercise of the powers of initiative and referendum under this charter.]

NOTE: Section 6.03 is in brackets because not all states provide for the initiative and referendum and it is possible that not all counties within the states that do provide for it will choose to include the option in their charters.

Article VII
GENERAL PROVISIONS

Section 7.01. Conflicts of Interest; Board of Ethics.

(a) **Conflicts of Interest.** The use of public office for private gain is prohibited. The county council shall implement this prohibition by ordinance. Regulations to this end shall include but not be limited to: acting in an official capacity on matters in which the official has a private financial interest clearly separate from that of the general public; the acceptance of gifts and other things of value; acting in a private capacity on matters dealt with as a public official, the use of confidential information; and appearances by county officials before other county agencies on behalf of private interests. This ordinance shall provide for reasonable public disclosure of finances by officials with major decision-making authority over monetary expenditures and contractual matters and, insofar as permissible under state law, shall provide for fines and imprisonment for violations.

(b) **Board of Ethics.** The county council shall, by ordinance, establish an independent board of ethics to administer and enforce the conflict of interest and financial disclosure ordinances. No member of the board may hold elective or appointive office under the county or any other government or hold any political party office. Insofar as possible under state law, the county council shall authorize the board to issue binding advisory opinions, conduct investigations on its own initiative and on referral or complaint, refer cases for prosecution, impose administrative fines, and to hire independent counsel. The county council shall appropriate sufficient funds to the board of ethics to enable it to perform the duties assigned to it.

Section 7.02. Prohibitions.
(a) Activities Prohibited.
(1) No person shall be appointed to or removed from, or in any way favored or discriminated against with respect to any county position or appointive county administrative office because of race, gender, age, handicap, religion, country of origin or political affiliation.

(2) No person shall willfully make any false statement, certificate, mark, rating or report in regard to any test, certification or appointment under the provisions of this charter or the rules and regulations made thereunder, or in any manner commit or attempt to commit any fraud preventing the impartial execution of such provisions, rules and regulations.

(3) No person who seeks appointment or promotion with respect to any county position or appointive county administrative office shall directly or indirectly give, render or pay any money, service or other valuable thing to any person for or in connection with his or her test, appointment, proposed appointment, promotion or proposed promotion.

(4) No person shall knowingly or willfully solicit or assist in soliciting any assessment, subscription or contribution for any political party or political purpose to be used in conjunction with any county election from any county employee.

(5) No county employee shall knowingly or willfully make, solicit or receive any contribution to the campaign funds of any political party or committee to be used in a county election or to campaign funds to be used in support of or opposition to any candidate for election to county office or county ballot issue. Further, no county employee shall knowingly or willfully participate in any aspect of any political campaign on behalf of or in opposition to any candidate for county office. This section

shall not be construed to limit any person's right to exercise rights as a citizen to express opinions or to cast a vote nor shall it be construed to prohibit any person from active participation in political campaigns at any other level of government.

(b) **Penalties.** Any person convicted of a violation of this section shall be ineligible for a period of five years following such conviction to hold any county office or position and, if an officer or employee of the county, shall immediately forfeit his or her office or position. The county council shall establish by ordinance such further penalties as it may deem appropriate.

Article VIII

CHARTER AMENDMENT

Section 8.01. Proposal of Amendment.

Amendments to this charter may be framed and proposed:

(a) In the manner provided by law, or

(b) By ordinance of the county council containing the full text of the proposed amendment and effective upon adoption, or

(c) By report of a charter commission created by ordinance; or

(d) By the voters of the county.

When any five qualified voters initiate proceedings to amend the charter by filing with the county clerk an affidavit stating they will constitute the petitioners' committee and be responsible for circulating the petition and filing it in proper form, stating their names and addresses and specifying the address to which all notices to the committee are to be sent, and setting out in full the proposed charter amendment. Promptly after the affidavit of the petitioners' committee is filed the clerk shall issue the appropriate petition blanks to the petitioners' committee. The petitions shall contain or have attached thereto throughout their circulation the full text of the proposed charter amendment and must be signed by registered voters of the county in the number of at least twenty percent of the total number of registered voters at the last regular county election. The petitioners' committee may withdraw the petition at any time before the fifteenth day immediately preceding the day scheduled for the county vote on the amendment.

Section 8.02. Election.

Upon delivery to the county election authorities of the report of a charter commission or delivery by the county clerk of an adopted ordinance proposing an amendment pursuant to §8.01(b) or a petition finally determined sufficient proposing an amendment pursuant to §8.01(d), the election authorities shall submit the proposed amendment to the voters of the county at an election. Such election shall be announced by a notice containing the complete text of the proposed amendment and published in one or more newspapers of general circulation in the county at least 30 days prior to the date of the election. If the amendment is proposed by petition, the amendment may be withdrawn at any time prior to the fifteenth day preceding the day scheduled for the election by filing with the county clerk a request for withdrawal signed by at least four members of the petitioners' committee. The election shall be held not less than 60 and not more than 120 days after the adoption of the ordinance or report, or the final determination of sufficiency of the petition proposing the amendment. If no regular election is to be held within that period, the county council shall provide for a special election on the proposed amendment; otherwise, the holding of a special election shall be as specified in the state election law.

Section 8.03. Adoption of Amendment.

If a majority of the registered voters of the county voting upon a proposed charter amendment vote in favor of it, the amendment shall become effective at the time fixed in the amendment or, if no time is therein fixed, 30 days after its adoption by the voters.

Article IX
TRANSITION/SEPARABILITY PROVISIONS

Section 9.01. Officers and Employees.

(a) **Rights and Privileges Preserved.** Nothing in this charter except as otherwise specifically provided shall affect or impair the rights or privileges of persons who are county officers or employees at the time of its adoption.

(b) **Continuance of Office or Employment.** Except as specifically provided by this charter, if at the time this charter takes full effect a county administrative officer or employee holds any office or position which is or can be abolished by or under this charter, he or she shall continue in such office or position until the taking effect of some specific provision under this charter directing that he or she vacate the office or position.

(c) **Personnel System.** An employee holding a county position at the time this charter takes full effect, who was serving in that same or a comparable position at the time of its adoption, shall not be subject to competitive tests as a condition of continuance in the same position but in all other respects shall be subject to the personnel system provided for in §4.02.

Section 9.02. Departments, Offices and Agencies.

(a) **Transfer of Powers.** If a county department, office or agency is abolished by this charter, the powers and duties given it by law shall be transferred to the county department, office or agency designated in this charter or, if the charter makes no provision, designated by the county council.

(b) **Property and Records.** All property, records and equipment of any department, office or agency existing when this charter is adopted shall be transferred to the department, office or agency assuming its powers and duties, but, in the event that the powers or duties are to be discontinued or divided between units or in the event that any conflict arises regarding a transfer, such property, records or equipment shall be transferred to one or more departments, offices or agencies designated by the county council in accordance with this charter.

Section 9.03. Pending Matters.

All rights, claims, actions, orders, contracts and legal administrative proceedings shall continue except as modified pursuant to the provisions of this charter and in each case shall be maintained, carried on or dealt with by the county department, office or agency appropriate under this charter.

Section 9.04. Laws in Force.

(a) **In General.** All county ordinances, resolutions, orders and regulations which are in force when this charter becomes fully effective are repealed to the extent that they are inconsistent or interfere with the effective operation of this charter or of ordinances or resolutions adopted pursuant thereto. To the extent that the constitution and laws of the state of _____ permit, all laws relating to or affecting this county or its agencies, officers or employees which are in force when this charter becomes fully effective are superseded to the extent that they are inconsistent or interfere with the effective operation of this charter or of ordinances or resolutions adopted pursuant thereto.

(b) **Specific Provisions.** Without limitation of the general operation of subsection (a) or of the number or nature of the provisions to which it applies:

(1) The following laws and parts of laws generally affecting counties or county agencies, officers or employees are inapplicable to the county of _____ or its agencies, officers or employees: [enumeration]

(2) The following public local laws relating to the county of _____ are superseded: [enumeration]

(3) The following ordinances, resolutions, orders and regulations of _____ [former county governing body] are repealed: [enumeration]

Section 9.05. Schedule.

(a) **First Election.** At the time of its adoption, this charter shall be in effect to the extent necessary in order that the first election of members of the county council may be conducted in accordance with the provisions of this charter. The first election shall be held on the _____ of _____. The _____ [county officials to be designated] shall prepare and adopt temporary regulations applicable only to the first election and designed to insure its proper conduct and to prevent fraud and provide for recount of ballots in cases of doubt or fraud.

(b) **Time of Taking Full Effect.** The charter shall be in full effect for all purposes on and after the date and time of the first meeting of the newly elected county council provided in §9.05(c).

(c) **First Council Meeting.** On the _____ of _____ following the first election of county council members under this charter, the newly elected members of the council shall meet at _____ [time] at _____ [place]:

(1) For the purpose of electing the [chairman and] vice chairman, appointing or considering the appointment of a county manager or acting county manager, and choosing, if it so desires, one of its members to act as temporary clerk pending appointment of a county clerk pursuant to §2.08; and
NOTE: Omit bracketed words if Section 2.03, Alternative II is used.

(2) For the purpose of adopting ordinances and resolutions necessary to effect the transition of government under this charter and to maintain effective county government during that transition.

(d) **Temporary Ordinances.** In adopting ordinances as provided in §9.05(c), the county council shall follow the procedures prescribed in Article II, except that at its first meeting or any meeting held within 60 days thereafter, the council may adopt temporary ordinances to deal with cases in which there is an urgent need for prompt action in connection with the transition of government and in which the delay incident to the appropriate ordinance procedure would probably cause serious hardship or impairment of effective county government. Every temporary ordinance shall be plainly labelled as such but shall be introduced in the form and manner prescribed for ordinances generally. A temporary ordinance may be considered and may be adopted with or without amendment or rejected at the meeting at which it is introduced. After adoption of a temporary ordinance, the council shall cause it to be printed and published as prescribed for other adopted ordinances. A temporary ordinance shall become effective upon adoption or at such later time preceding automatic repeal under this subsection as it may specify[, and the referendum power shall not extend to any such ordinance]. Every temporary ordinance, including any amendments made thereto after adoption, shall automatically stand repealed as of the 91st day following the date on which it was adopted, renewed or otherwise continued except by adoption in the manner prescribed in Article II for ordinances of the kind concerned.

(e) **Initial Expenses.** The initial expenses of the county council, including the expense of recruiting a county manager, shall be paid by the county on vouchers signed by the council chairman.

(f) **Initial Salary of Council Chairman and Council Members.** The chairman of the council shall receive an annual salary in the amount of $_____ and each other council member in the amount of $_____, until such amount is changed by the council in accordance with the provisions of this charter.

Section 9.06. Separability.

If any provision of this charter is held invalid, the other provisions of the charter shall not be affected thereby. If the application of the charter or any of its provisions to any person or circumstance is held invalid, the application of the charter and its provisions to other persons or circumstances shall not be affected thereby.

– – – –

Editor's Note: A complete copy of this document may be obtained from the National Civic League, 1445 Market Street, Suite 300, Denver, Colorado 80202-1717, telephone (303) 571-4343.

Notes

1. H.S. Gilbertson, "The Dark Continent of American Politics," in *The County* (New York: The National Short Ballot Organization, 1917).

2. Clyde Snider, "American County Government: A Midcentury Review," *American Political Science Review* 46 (March 1952): 74.

3. 1987 Census of Governments (GC87-1CP), November 1987, 1.

4. Herbert S. Duncombe, *Modern County Government* (Washington, D.C.: National Association of Counties, 1977): 20.

5. National Association of Counties (telephone interview with Research Department), 15 November 1988.

6. Duncombe, 51.

7. Tanis Salant, "County Home Rule: Perspectives for Decision Making in Arizona," in *County Issues* (University of Arizona, 1988), 10.

8. Florence Zeller, "Forms of County Government," in *County Year Book* (Washington, D.C.: International City Management Association, 1975), 28.

9. Joe Zimmerman, "Transfers of Functional Responsibilities," in *County Year Book* (Washington, D.C.: International City Management Association, 1976), 59.

10. Harry P. Hatry and Carl F. Valente, "Alternative Service Delivery Approaches Involving Increased Use of the Private Sector," in *The Municipal Year Book* (Washington, D.C.: International City Management Association, 1983), 201.

11. Salant, 41.

12. Alistair McArthur, "3,049 Labs for Local Government Testing," *Public Management* (April 1971): 3.

13. From *America's Counties Today 1973* (Washington, D.C.: National Association of Counties, 1973).

14. Zeller, 28.

15. *County Government Finances in 1985–1986*, U.S. Bureau of Census, 1988, 1.

16. Kim Beury, "Counties Hopeful for New Deal," *American City and County* (August 1988): 31.

17. *County Government Finances in 1979–1980*, U.S. Bureau of Census, 1981, 5.

Regional Government

Bruce D. McDowell

What Is Regionalism?

The United States is a nation of regions. Some are big, like the major river basins, the cornbelt, the sunbelt, the frostbelt, and the northeastern megalopolis. Some are small, like the 300 or so metropolitan areas and the numerous rural commutersheds defined by the federal government. Some cross state lines, while others are in one state. Even among the "small" areas, there are about three dozen interstate metropolitan areas that cross state lines, greatly increasing their governmental complexity.

Each region has problems and opportunities that its citizens and governments strive to address. Yet most are not governed as single units; they span the jurisdictions of many governments.

The most common means of coping with these regions' issues has been to establish regional planning commissions or councils to study pressing problems and advise local, state, and federal agencies about potential remedies. In the American experience, these planning bodies almost always have been advisory only — without the power to govern by themselves. If

Originally published as "Regionalism: What It Is, Where We Are, and Where We May Be Headed," The Regionalist, Vol. 1, No. 4, Spring, 1996. Published by the National Association of Regional Councils, Washington, D.C. Reprinted with permission of the publisher.

they cannot convince the regularly constituted local, state, and federal authorities to act on their recommendations, those recommendations simply sit on a shelf somewhere — until there is another study, another set of recommendations, and another opportunity to persuade the regular governments to act — often against their own individual self-interests.

Exceptions to this general pattern are so rare that they draw immediate, excited, and hopeful attention. Some of the most prominent examples of authoritative regional bodies are

- Tennessee Valley Authority;
- Susquehanna and Delaware River Basin Commissions;
- Metropolitan Service District in Portland, Oregon;
- Twin Cities Metropolitan Council in Minnesota; and
- Metropolitan Transportation Commission in San Francisco/Oakland, California.

But then they usually are dismissed as special cases, not appropriate for replication anywhere else. They were the product of a unique set of circumstances that required emergency action that is not justified in a normal situation.

In contrast, the advisory regions abound. It is just too local and politically attractive to have an organization that can geographically "get its arms around the problem." Since many regional problems deserve this degree the recognition, many regional organizations have been created, and many of them lie on top of each other.

Where We Are and How We Got There

In the early part of this century, there was great excitement about regional solutions to governmental problems. Much of it was pushed along by planners, political scientists, public administrators, economists, water resources professionals, and the "good government" movement that brought so many other reforms to government during that period. And, from about 1920 until about 1960, there was a great deal of experimentation with regional planning commissions, statewide planning, and river basin commissions. By 1960, these organizations spotted the continent at wide intervals and whetted the public's appetite for more.

THE 1960S AND 1970S

The 1960s and 1970s saw the nation almost completely covered both by multistate river basin and economic development commissions that had state and federal participation and by metropolitan and nonmetropolitan regional councils dominated by local government officials. Most of the metropolitan and nonmetropolitan regional councils were carefully designed to be "areawide" according to some criteria — such as commutersheds or areas of interdependent economic influences. By the end of the 1970s, 99 percent of all the nation's counties (or county areas in New England) were participating in regional councils.

This explosion of areawide regional councils and multistate river basin and economic development regions occurred because of very intentional and systematic federal action that drew in states as well as local governments. In the cases of the areawide councils, the federal action established thirty-nine grant programs designed to require and fund regional planning, and it appealed directly to the governors of all fifty states to establish statewide systems of "substate districts" to systematize the administration of the federal programs that support regional councils. And many of the states did so.

By 1977, the area wide regions spurred by federal programs were so pervasive and so firmly established that the Census of Governments taken that year included a special report on them. The census found 675 general purpose (or multipurpose) regional councils and 1,257 special purpose regional organizations serving federal program purposes. On average across the nation, the general purpose regional councils were designated to carry out 3.73 federal programs, while the special purpose ones generally carried out a single federal program.

In the Southwest and Appalachia, the general purpose regions were designated to handle more than five of the federal government's regional programs together. The federal government strongly supported multiple designations, but the states had a lot to do with making some of these designations and they took differing approaches. Some states reinforced the federal policy of multiple designations, while others did not.

During the golden age of regional organizations in America, the federal government was committed to the idea that regional planning could help solve many of the nation's urban, rural, economic development, environmental, and water resources problems. Federal funds for regional planning flowed freely throughout the country, and the regional bodies prepared many planning studies, yielding comprehensive regional plans with an array of specific functional elements and multiyear action programs.

The federal funds supplied the big bucks in the budgets of most regional planning organizations— often up to 75 percent. And the accompanying federal planning requirements defined the type of planning that was done.

THE 1980S

The 1980s tell a very different story. The federal government abandoned most of its commitment to regionalism. Of the thirty-nine programs designed and enacted during the preceding two decades to promote regional organizations, only one — metropolitan transportation planning — remained relatively unscathed by this sudden reversal of federal policy. By 1984, the rest had been terminated, substantially defunded, or relieved of their region-promoting features. Most of this decline had occurred by 1982.

For the multistate programs, which had created most river basin and economic development regions by agreements between the governors and the president, President Reagan withdrew his approval, left them unfunded, and watched them die. The only ones that survived were those that had been created directly by federal law or interstate compact.

The metropolitan and nonmetropolitan areawide councils rapidly lost federal designations and funding. By 1984, their budgets and staffs had been reduced by about half. Their functions were beginning to migrate away from the federal government's areawide planning agenda to activities more in tune with services for which local governments, who were starting to pick up the funding responsibilities dropped by the feds, were willing to pay.

By the end of the 1980s, 80 percent of the areawide regional councils still existed, but they had changed dramatically. They were beginning to rebuild as data sharing, joint services, and regional service bodies. Even the councils still designated for metropolitan transportation and planning saw a decline — the land-use elements formerly funded by the Department of Housing and Urban Development and the environmental planning for wastewater treatment and air quality formerly funded by the Environmental Protection Agency had to be absorbed by DOT funds, which were at the same time being stretched thinner by the addition of a large number of new urban area designations following the 1980 census.

The federal economic development and Appalachian programs, though suffering significant cutbacks, managed to survive, maintaining some planning and other support to many of the nonmetropolitan regional councils. Thus, the federal abandonment of regions, though drastic, was not complete.

Through the 1980s, as the areawide councils struggled to adjust to the decline in federal support and raised their local government dues, state support remained almost as it had been. The state support, of course, differed greatly from one state to another at the beginning of the 1980s, and that remains true today. In those few states that provide direct financial support to the regional councils and rely on them for delivering federal and state programs, the councils have been somewhat insulated from the federal abandonment, but the number of states taking this position did not change much in response to the federal action. Independently, those few states that enacted new growth management programs during the 1980s tended to give additional important roles to their regional councils.

THE 1990s

In 1995, we cannot write the whole story of the 1990s. But we can begin.

The most significant occurrence so far has been the enactment of the Intermodal Surface Transportation Efficiency Act of 1991 (ISTEA). For those metropolitan planning organizations (MPOs) designated to satisfy ISTEA planning requirements (about 47 percent of which are areawide metropolitan regional councils), the federal funding and expectations have increased significantly. But, the clear consensus is that the increase in expectations has been greater than the increase in funding.

Before discussing this development further, it is significant to note that about *75 percent* of the MPOs had been areawide regional councils in the mid–1970s when the federal government was intentionally supporting those organizations.

A recent U.S. Advisory Commission on Intergovernmental Relations (ACIR) study of the capacity of MPOs to meet the expectations of ISTEA turned up mixed results.

A broad range of participants in eighteen MPOs across the country agreed that ISTEA had brought about many desirable changes, including the following:

- increased public participation,
- more air quality planning,
- better intergovernmental coordination,
- better relationships between the state department of transportation and the MPO,
- new or increased attention to intermodal issues, and
- new or increased attention to long-range planning.

But, these same interview respondents identified many difficulties they were encountering:

- increased regulatory and workload burdens,
- unachievable expectations,
- uncoordinated deadlines among the various federal requirements and between the federal requirements and related state and local requirements,
- disrupted relationships within the MPO, and
- new strains in the MPO relationship with the state DOT.

Of course, great differences exist from one state to another, and these findings are generalizations from cases that spanned the country.

Nevertheless, the bottom line of ACIR's *MPO Capacity* study, released in May 1995, was that MPOs need a lot of help to keep up with the great expectations of ISTEA. The challenges they face are institutional, technical, and political — and the political ones were seen by all as the most difficult. ACIR recommended a comprehensive capacity-building program for MPOs, but the political part deserves special note.

The MPOs are intergovernmental **processes**, not governments. But ISTEA assumes that they are governments with strong independent decision-making powers capable of speaking with a single voice for all local governments in the region and competing on an equal footing with the power of the governor, the state DOT, and a variety of federal and state agencies. In reality, even the best of the MPOs are lucky to be able to bring all these parties together to reach a modicum of consensus on a few of the key issues.

The MPOs, of course, must help themselves. No one can perform their roles for them. Striving for excellence in everything they do should be their first priority.

Nevertheless, they cannot do it alone. And, on the key political power issue, state support is crucial. ISTEA sets the MPOs in a mutual veto situation with the governor, the state DOT, and the air quality agency — and the MPO's veto is the weakest one by far. If the MPO process gets to the veto stage, it is probably a failure. Therefore, it is essential for all parties to use the MPO process as a good-faith bargaining forum in which everyone tries as hard as they can to reach consensus and to adhere to the agreements reached there.

Where We May Be Headed

Not much indicates that the multistate regions are on their way back. The only hint I have seen of that is the proposal in Congress to replace the Economic Development Administration (EDA) in the Department of Commerce with a series of eight regional commissions— modeled after the Appalachian Regional Commission (ARC). These multistate regions, with a federal co-chair, would make grants to the metropolitan and non-metropolitan areawide regions in economically depressed parts of the country, as EDA does now. But this proposal is not expected to pass. Meanwhile, there are continuing proposals to do away with ARC itself— proposals that must be continuously defended against, year after year.

At the areawide level, there may be two different tracks— one for MPOs and one for the majority of regional councils that are not MPOs. The MPOs now have a strengthened federal planning role, and they may be able to make something of it *if* the state DOTs let them. The other areawide regional councils appear headed for a much more limited local services role — a non-planning role. But both of these tracks are quite uncertain.

On the MPO track, the state DOTs already have signaled that they will challenge the enhanced roles for MPOs in ISTEA when that law comes up for renewal next year. The recently adopted policies of the American Association of State Highway and Transportation Officials (AASHTO)— spurred by the thirty-one Republican governors—call for cutting back on the planning funds for many of the MPOs and giving special weight to the planning of only the MPOs with populations of one million or more. If the state does not see that its own success is tightly linked to the success of all of its MPOs, then the MPOs probably will not be able to do what ISTEA expects. And there is little likelihood that the federal government will step in to save the MPOs in the current political environment, which is leaning heavily toward giving the states greater leeway in determining their own policies.

For the other regional councils, the local services function is one that increasingly will not attract federal or state funding. So it will have to be justified primarily on the basis of saving money for the local governments. Activities of that type — joint purchasing; shared personnel, equipment, data, and technical services— are important, but they leave the most significant regional issues untouched: issues such as infrastructure, the environment, and the social and economic disparities between inner cities and suburbs. The local consensus approach cannot deal with controversy unless there is also some outside-the-region mechanism for forcing the tougher issues to be confronted.

So, where should we look for hope of a better region? I have three suggestions for you to ponder:

• the business community,

• reality, and

• benchmarking.

THE BUSINESS COMMUNITY

In the Washington area, the Board of Trade has taken a hand in pushing for (1) a solution to the Woodrow Wilson Bridge replacement — a three-state facility on the area's only beltway, which is too narrow, has a draw-span that opens too much, and is in danger of collapse from overuse; (2) thinking more generally about the region's gridlocked transportation problems; and (3) marketing the whole region as a good place to do business. It also has taken the lead in convening joint meetings of public and private leaders to explore key public policy issues together. There is nothing earthshaking here, except that it does show a recognition that businesses operate throughout the whole region and have more on their minds than the concerns of the individual localities.

REALITY

Sooner or later, reality will catch up with us, and something will have to be done. The Woodrow Wilson Bridge may actually fall down. The beltway may actually grind to a halt. Regional problems are not imaginary.

They do make a difference in the lives of people, and they demand response — however ad hoc that response may be.

BENCHMARKING

The way to make the federal, state, and local governments accountable to the people and regain the people's trust and confidence is to set quantified goals, devise methods of measuring progress toward them, and report their status back to the people to show that they are actually getting something for the taxes they pay. This "benchmarking" system sets up a new kind of public dialogue about the effect governmental activities have in the lives of real people. Is the environment getting cleaner? Is congestion easing? Are our lives getting safer?

San Diego's growth management process is designed around such a "quality of life" performance measurement system. We should watch to see whether it makes a difference in restoring people's confidence in their governments. If it does, we may have another path open to us for helping to solve regional problems.

Conclusion

I wish the future were more clear for those of you following the regional path. The only real advice I can give you is to keep at it. We need regional approaches to regional problems, because regional problems are real. Sooner or later, our approaches to these problems will get real, and you will be there to lead the way.

– – – –

Editor's Note: The charter of the Metropolitan Service District (Metro) was selected as the "model" charter since it is the only regional government in the U.S. with a home-rule charter and directly elected officials. It is also known as one of the most progressive regional government organizations throughout the country.

The Metro serves more than 1.3 million residents of Clackamas, Multnomah, and Washington counties, and the 24 cities in the Portland, Oregon, metropolitan area.

MODEL REGIONAL GOVERNMENT CHARTER
Metro Charter Committee

Introduction

Filed by the Metro Charter Committee with the elections officer of the Portland area metropolitan service district, pursuant to ORS 268.730, and approved by district voters at the November 7, 1992 general election as amended by district voters at the November 7, 2000 general election.

PREAMBLE

We, the people of the Portland area metropolitan service district, in order to establish an elected, visible and accountable regional government that is responsive to the citizens of the region and works cooperatively with our local governments; that undertakes, as its most important service, planning and policy making to preserve and enhance the quality of life and the environment for ourselves and future generations; and that provides regional services needed and desired by the citizens in an efficient and effective manner, do ordain this charter for the Portland area metropolitan service district, to be known as Metro.

CHAPTER I — NAMES AND BOUNDARIES

Section 1. Title of Charter.
The title of this charter is the 1992 Metro Charter.

Section 2. Name of Regional Government.
The Portland area metropolitan service district, referred to in this charter as the "Metropolitan Service District," continues under this charter as a metropolitan service district with the name "Metro."

Section 3. Boundaries.
The Metro area of governance includes all territory within the boundaries of the Metropolitan Service District on the effective date of this charter and any territory later annexed or subjected to Metro governance under state law. This charter refers to that area as the "Metro area." Changes of Metro boundaries are not effective unless approved by ordinance. No change of Metro boundaries requires approval by a local government

boundary commission or any other state agency unless required by law. The custodian of Metro records shall keep an accurate description of Metro boundaries and make it available for public inspection.

CHAPTER II — FUNCTIONS AND POWERS

Section 4. Jurisdiction of Metro.
Metro has jurisdiction over matters of the powers of metropolitan concern. Matters of metropolitan concern include the powers granted to and duties imposed on Metro by current and future state law and those matters the council by ordinance determines to be of metropolitan concern. The council shall specify by ordinance the extent to which Metro exercises jurisdiction over matters of metropolitan concern.

Section 5. Regional Planning Functions.
(1) Future Vision.

   (a) Adoption. The council shall adopt a Future Vision for the region between January 15, 1995 and July 1, 1995. The Future Vision is a conceptual statement that indicates population levels and settlement patterns that the region can accommodate within the carrying capacity of the land, water and air resources of the region, and its educational and economic resources, and that achieves a desired quality of life. The Future Vision is a long-term, visionary outlook for at least a 50-year period. As used in this section, "region" means the Metro area and adjacent areas.

   (b) Matters addressed. The matters addressed by the Future Vision include but are not limited to: (a) use, restoration and preservation of regional land and natural resources for the benefit of present and future generations; (2) how and where to accommodate the population growth for the region while maintaining a desired quality of life for its residents; and (3) how to develop new communities and additions to the existing urban areas in well-planned ways.

   (c) Development. The council shall appoint a commission to develop and recommend a proposed Future Vision by a date the council sets. The commission shall be broadly representative of both public and private sectors, including the academic community, in the region. At least one member must reside outside the Metro area. The commission has authority to seek any necessary information and shall consider all relevant information and public comment in developing the proposed Future Vision. The commission serves without compensation.

(d) Review and amendment. The Future Vision may be reviewed and amended as provided by ordinance. The Future Vision shall be completely reviewed and revised at least every fifteen years in the manner specified in subsection (1)(c) of this section.

(e) Effect. The Future Vision is not a regulatory document. It is the intent of this charter that the Future Vision have no effect that would allow court or agency review of it.

(2) Regional Framework Plan.

(a) Adoption. The council shall adopt a regional framework plan by December 31, 1997 with the consultation and advice of the Metro Policy Advisory Committee (MPAC) created under section 27 of this charter. The council may adopt the regional framework plan in components.

(b) Matters addressed. The regional framework plan shall address: (1) regional transportation and mass transit systems; (2) management and amendment of the urban growth boundary; (3) protection of lands outside the urban growth boundary for natural resource, future urban or other uses; (4) housing densities, (5) urban design and settlement patterns; (6) parks, open spaces and recreational facilities; (7) water sources and storage; (8) coordination, to the extent feasible, of Metro growth management and land use planning policies with those of Clark County, Washington; and (9) planning responsibilities mandated by state law. The regional framework plan shall also address other growth management and land use planning matters which the council, with the consultation and advice of the MPAC, determines are of metropolitan concern and will benefit from regional planning. To encourage regional uniformity, the regional framework plan shall also contain model terminology, standards and procedures for local land use decision making that may be adopted by local governments. As used in this section, "local" refers only to the cities and counties within the jurisdiction of Metro.

(c) Effect. The regional framework plan shall: (1) describe its relationship to the Future Vision; (2) comply with applicable statewide planning goals; (3) be subject to compliance acknowledgment by the Land Conservation and Development Commission or its successor; and (4) be the basis for coordination of local comprehensive plans and implementing regulations.

(d) Amendment. The council may amend the regional framework plan after seeking the consultation and advice of the MPAC.

(e) Implementation. To the maximum extent allowed by law, the council shall adopt ordinances: (1) requiring local comprehensive plans and implementing regulations to comply with the regional framework plan within three years after adoption of the entire regional framework plan. If the regional framework plan is subject to compliance acknowledgment, local plans and implementing regulations shall be required to comply with the regional framework plan within two years of compliance acknowledgment; (2) requiring the council to adjudicate and determine the consistency of local comprehensive plans with the regional framework plan; (3) requiring each city and county within the jurisdiction of Metro to make local land use decisions consistent with the regional framework plan until its comprehensive plan has been determined to be consistent with the regional framework plan. The obligation to apply the regional framework plan to local land use decisions shall not begin until one year after adoption and compliance acknowledgment of the regional framework plan; and (4) allowing the council to require changes in local land use standards and procedures if the council determines changes are necessary to remedy a pattern or practice of decision making inconsistent with the regional framework plan.

(3) Priority and funding of regional planning activities. The regional planning functions under this section are the primary functions of Metro. The council shall appropriate funds sufficient to assure timely completion of those functions.

Section 6. Other Assigned Functions.
Other Assigned Functions. Metro is also authorized to exercise the following functions: (1) Acquisition, development, maintenance and operation of: (a) a metropolitan zoo, (b) public cultural, trade, convention, exhibition, sports, entertainment, and spectator facilities, (c) facilities for the disposal of solid and liquid wastes, and (d) a system of parks, open spaces and recreational facilities of metropolitan concern; (2) disposal of solid and liquid wastes; (3) metropolitan aspects of natural disaster planning and response coordination; (4) development and marketing of data; and (5) any other function required by state law or assigned to the Metropolitan Service District or Metro by the voters.

Section 7. Assumption of Additional Functions.
(1) Assumption ordinance. The council shall approve by ordinance the undertaking by Metro of any function not authorized by sections 5 and 6 of this charter. The ordinance shall contain a finding that the function is of metropolitan concern and the reasons it is appropriate for Metro to undertake it.

(2) Assumption of local government service function.

  (a) An ordinance authorizing provision or regulation by Metro of a local government service is not effective unless the ordinance is approved by the voters of Metro or a majority of the members of the MPAC. Voter approval may occur by approval of a referred measure (1) authorizing the function or (2) relating to finances and authorizing financing or identifying funds to be used for exercise of the function. As used in this section, "local government service" is a service provided to constituents by one or more cities, counties or special districts within the jurisdiction of Metro at the time a Metro ordinance on assumption of the service is first introduced.
  (b) An ordinance submitted to the MPAC for approval is deemed approved unless disapproved within 60 days after submission.
  (c) No approval under this subsection is required for the compensated provision of services by Metro to or on behalf of a local government under an agreement with that government.

(3) Assumption of other service functions. The council shall seek the advice of the MPAC before adopting an ordinance authorizing provision or regulation by Metro of a service, which is not a local government service.

(4) Assumption of functions and operations of mass transit district. Notwithstanding subsection (2) of this section, Metro may at any time assume the duties, functions, powers and operations of a mass transit district by ordinance. Before adoption of this ordinance the council shall seek the advice of the Joint Policy Advisory Committee on Transportation or its successor. After assuming the functions and operations of a mass transit district, the council shall establish a mass transit commission of not fewer than seven members and determine its duties in administering mass transit functions for Metro. The members of the governing body of the mass transit district at the time of its assumption by Metro are members of the initial Metro mass transit commission for the remainder of their respective terms of office.

(5) Boundary commission functions. The council shall undertake and complete a study of the Portland Metropolitan Area Local Government Boundary Commission, with advice of the MPAC, by September 1, 1995. The council shall implement the results of the study and shall seek any legislative action needed for implementation.

Section 8. Preservation of Authority to Contract.

All Metro officers shall preserve, to the greatest extent possible, the ability of Metro to contract for all services with persons or entities who are not Metro employees.

Section 9. General Grant of Powers to Carry Out Functions; Construction of Specified Powers.

When carrying out the functions authorized or assumed under this charter: (1) Metro has all powers that the laws of the United States and this state now or in the future could allow Metro just as if this charter specifically set out each of those powers; (2) the powers specified in this charter are not exclusive; (3) any specification of power in this charter is not intended to limit authority; and (4) the powers specified in this charter shall be construed liberally.

CHAPTER III — FINANCE

Section 10. General Authority.

Except as prohibited by law or restricted by this charter, Metro may impose, levy and collect taxes and may issue revenue bonds, general and special obligation bonds, certificates of participation and other obligations. The authority provided under this section supplements any authority otherwise granted by law.

Section 11. Voter Approval of Certain Taxes.

Any ordinance of the council imposing broadly based taxes of general applicability on the personal income, business income, payroll, property, or sales of goods or services of all, or a number of classes of, persons or entities in the region requires approval of the voters of Metro before taking effect. This approval is not required (1) to continue property taxes imposed by the Metropolitan Service District, (2) for the rate or amount of any payroll tax imposed by a mass transit district as of June 1, 1992, if the functions of that district are assumed by Metro, or (3) for additional payroll tax revenues for mass transit imposed to replace revenues lost by withdrawal of any locality from the service area of the mass transit district after June 1, 1992. For purposes of sections 11, 13, and 14 of this charter, "taxes" do not include any user charge, service fee, franchise fee, charge for the issuance of any franchise, license, permit or approval, or any benefit assessment against property.

Section 12. Voter Approval of General Obligation Bonds.
Issuance of general obligation bonds payable from ad valorem property taxes requires the approval of the voters of Metro.

Section 13. Prior Consultation for Tax Imposition.
Before imposing any new tax for which voter approval is not required, the council shall establish and seek the advice of a tax study committee that includes members appointed from the general population, and from among businesses and the governments of cities, counties, special districts and school districts, of the Metro area.

Section 14. Limitations on Expenditures of Certain Tax Revenues.
(1) Generally. Except as provided in this section, for the first fiscal year after this charter takes effect Metro may make no more than $12,500,000 in expenditures on a cash basis from taxes imposed and received by Metro and interest and other earnings on those taxes. This expenditure limitation increases in each subsequent fiscal year by a percentage equal to (a) the rate of increase in the Consumer Price Index, All Items, for Portland-Vancouver (All Urban Consumers) as determined by the appropriate federal agency or (b) the most nearly equivalent index as determined by the council if the index described in (a) is discontinued.

(2) Exclusions from limitation. This section does not apply to (a) taxes approved by the voters of Metro or the Metropolitan Service District and interest and other earnings on those taxes, (b) payroll taxes specified in Section 11 of this charter, and (c) tax increment financing charges on property.

Section 15. Limitations on Amount of User Charges.
Except to the extent receipts in excess of costs from food and beverage sales, parking and other concessions are dedicated to reducing charges for the provision of goods or services to which the concession directly relates, charges for the provision of goods or services by Metro may not exceed the costs of providing the goods or services. These costs include, but are not limited to, costs of personal services, materials, capital outlay, debt

service, operating expenses, overhead expenses, and capital and operational reserves attributable to the goods or services.

CHAPTER IV — FORM OF GOVERNMENT

Section 16. Metro Council.
(1) Creation and Powers. The Metro council is created as the governing body of Metro. Except as this charter provides otherwise, and except for initiative and referendum powers reserved to the voters of Metro, all Metro powers are vested in the council.

(2) Composition. Beginning January 6, 2003, the council consists of seven (7) councilors, one of whom shall be elected at large and designated President of the council and six (6) each nominated and elected from a single district within the Metro area. Until that date the council consists of the seven (7) members of the Metro Council whose terms begin or continue in January 2001 and whose districts continue until replaced.

(3) Initial terms of office. The terms of office of the four councilors receiving the highest number of votes among the seven councilors elected in 1994 end January 4, 1999. The terms of office of the other three councilors end January 6, 1997. Thereafter the term of office of councilor is four years.

(4) Presiding Officer, Council President.

  (a) Presiding Officer. At its first meeting each year before 2003, the council shall elect a presiding officer from its councilors.
  (b) Council President. The Council President presides over the Council. The Council President sets the council agenda subject to general rules established by a council adopted ordinance. Except as provided otherwise by the Metro Charter, the Council President appoints all members of the committees, commissions and boards created by the rules of the council and ordinances of Metro.

(5) Annual Organizing Resolution. At the first Council meeting each January the Council shall adopt an annual organizing resolution naming a deputy and establishing such committees as the Council deems necessary for the orderly conduct of council business.

(6) Council meetings. The council shall meet regularly in the Metro area at times and places it designates. The council shall prescribe by ordinance the rules to govern conduct of its meetings. Except as this charter provides

otherwise, the agreement of a majority of councilors present and constituting a quorum is necessary to decide affirmatively a question before the council.

(7) Quorum. A majority of councilors in office is a quorum for council business, but fewer councilors may compel absent councilors to attend.

(8) Record of proceedings. The council shall keep and authenticate a record of council proceedings.

Section 17. Metro Executive Officer.
(1) Creation. The office of Metro executive officer is created. The executive officer is elected from the Metro area at large for a term of four years. The executive officer serves full time and may not be employed by any other person or entity while serving as executive officer.

(2) Duties. The primary duty of the executive officer is to enforce Metro ordinances and otherwise to execute the policies of the council. The executive officer shall also: (a) administer Metro except for the council and the auditor; (b) make appointments to Metro offices boards, commissions and committees when required to do so by this charter or by ordinance; (c) propose for council adoption measures deemed necessary to enforce or carry out powers and duties of Metro; (d) prepare and submit a recommended annual Metro budget to the council for approval; and (e) keep the council fully advised about Metro operations.

(3) Transition from Metropolitan Service District. The Metropolitan Service District executive officer in office when this charter takes effect is the Metro executive officer until January 2, 1995 when his or her term expires. The Metro executive officer is elected in the first statewide primary or general election after adoption of this charter for a term beginning January 2, 1995.

(4) Veto.

   (a) Except as provided in this subsection, the executive officer may veto the following legislative acts of the council within five business days after enactment: (1) any annual or supplemental Metro budget, (2) any ordinance imposing, or providing an exception from, a tax, and (3) any ordinance imposing a charge for provision of goods, services or property by Metro, franchise fees or any assessment.

(b) The council, not later than 30 days after a veto, may override a veto by the affirmative vote of (1) nine councilors while the council consists of 13 positions and (2) five councilors after the council consists of seven positions as provided by section 16(2) of this charter.

(c) A legislative act referred to the voters of Metro by the council is not subject to veto.

(5) Office Abolished. Effective January 6, 2003, the office of the Executive Officer is abolished.

(6) Section 17 Repealed. Section 17 of the Metro Charter is repealed January 6, 2003. Upon repeal, its provisions shall be stricken from the Metro Charter.

Section 18. Metro Auditor.
(1) Creation. The office of Metro auditor is created. The auditor is elected from the Metro area at large for a term of four years. The auditor serves full time and may not be employed by any other person or entity while serving as auditor.

(2) First election; disqualification for other Metro elected offices. The auditor is first elected in the first statewide primary or general election after adoption of this charter for a term beginning January 2, 1995. During the term for which elected, and for four years thereafter, the auditor is ineligible to hold the office of Metro councilor.

(3) Duties. The auditor shall: (a) make continuous investigations of the operations of Metro including financial and performance auditing and review of financial transactions, personnel, equipment, facilities, and all other aspects of those operations, and (b) make reports to the Metro council of the results of any investigation with any recommendations for remedial action. Except as provided in this section, the auditor may not be given responsibility to perform any executive function.

Section 19. Term of Office.
The term of office of an officer elected at a primary or general election begins the first Monday of the year following election and continues until a successor assumes the office.

CHAPTER V — OFFICERS, COMMISSIONS, AND EMPLOYEES

Section 20. Qualifications of Elected Officers.
(1) Councilor. A councilor shall be a qualified elector under the constitu-

tion of this state when his or her term of office begins and shall have resided during the preceding 12 months in the district from which elected or appointed. When the boundaries of that district have been apportioned or reapportioned during that period, residency in that district for purposes of this subsection includes residency in any former district with area in the district from which the councilor is elected or appointed if residence is established in the apportioned or reapportioned district within 60 days after the apportionment or reapportionment is effective.

(2) Council President and auditor. The Council President and auditor shall each be a qualified elector under the constitution of this state when his or her term of office begins and shall have resided during the preceding 12 months within the boundaries of Metro as they exist when the term of office begins. At the time of election or appointment, the auditor shall also hold the designation of certified public accountant or certified internal auditor.

3) Multiple elected offices. A Metro elected officer may not be an elected officer of the state, or a city, county or special district during his or her term of office. As used in this charter, special district does not include school districts.

(4) Judging elections and qualifications. The council is the judge of the election and qualification of its members.

Section 21. Compensation of Elected Officers.
(1) Council. Prior to 2003, the salary of the presiding officer is two-thirds the salary of a circuit court judge of this state and the salary of every other councilor is one-third the salary of a circuit court judge of this state. Beginning January 6, 2003, the salary of the Council President shall be that of a circuit court judge of this state and the salary of every other councilor is one-third the salary of a circuit court judge. A councilor may waive a salary.

(2) Executive officer. Until the office is abolished, the salary of the executive officer is the salary of a circuit court judge of this state.

(3) Auditor. The salary of the auditor is eighty percent of the salary of a circuit court judge of this state.

(4) Full Compensation. Elected officers compensation, as established by this charter, shall be the elected officers full and exclusive compensation for their duties as Metro officers or for any duties or responsibilities result-

ing from their position. This Section does not preclude elected officers from receiving ordinary employee fringe benefits or being reimbursed for any actual and reasonable expenses incurred by an elected officer in the course of performing official duties.

Section 22. Oath.
Before assuming office a Metro elected officer shall take an oath or affirm that he or she will faithfully perform the duties of the office and support the constitutions and laws of the United States and this state and the charter and laws of Metro.

Section 23. Vacancies in Office.
(1) Councilor. The office of councilor becomes vacant upon the incumbent's: (a) death, (b) adjudicated incompetency, (c) recall from office, (d) failure following election or appointment to qualify for the office within 10 days after the time for his or her term of office to begin, (e) absence from all meetings of the council within a 60 day period without the council's consent, (f) ceasing to reside in the district from which elected or appointed, except when district boundaries are reapportioned and a councilor is assigned to a district where the councilor does not reside and the councilor becomes a resident of the reapportioned district within 60 days after the reapportionment is effective, (g) ceasing to be a qualified elector under state law, (h) conviction of a felony or conviction of a federal or state offense punishable by loss of liberty and pertaining to his or her office, (i) resignation from office, or (j) becoming an elected officer of the state or a city, county or special district.

(2) Council President and auditor. The offices of Council President or auditor become vacant in the circumstances described in subsection (a)–(d) and (g)–(j) of this section, or if the Council President or auditor ceases to reside in the Metro area. The office of auditor also becomes vacant if the incumbent ceases to hold the designation of certified public accountant or certified internal auditor.

(3) Vacancy after reapportionment. If a councilor vacancy occurs after the councilor has been assigned to a reapportioned district under section 32 of this charter, the vacancy is in the district to which that councilor was assigned.

(4) Determination of vacancy. The council is the final judge of the existence of a vacancy.

Section 24. Filling Vacancies.

A majority of councilors holding office shall fill a vacancy by appointment within 90 days after it occurs. The term of office of the appointee runs from the time he or she qualifies for the office after appointment until a successor is duly elected and qualifies for the office. If the vacancy occurs more than 20 days before the first general election after the beginning of the term for that office, the term of office of the appointee runs only until the first council meeting in the year immediately after that election. A person shall be elected for the remainder of the term at the first primary or general election after the beginning of the term.

Section 25. Limitations of Terms of Office.

No person may be elected councilor for more than three consecutive full terms, not including any term or terms as Council President. No person may be elected Council President for more than two consecutive full terms. Any term served as Executive Officer shall be considered as a term served as Council President. The limitations of this section apply only to terms of office beginning on or after January 2, 1995.

Section 26. Appointive Offices and Commissions.

(1) Chief Operating Officer. The Council shall provide by ordinance for the creation of the office of the Chief Operating Officer. The Chief Operating Officer's duties and responsibilities will be more specifically established by ordinance. The Council President appoints the Chief Operating Officer subject to confirmation by the Council. The Chief Operating Officer serves at the pleasure of the Council and is subject to removal by the Council President with the concurrence of the Council.

(2) Metro Attorney. The Council shall provide by ordinance for the creation of the office of Metro Attorney. The Council President appoints the Metro Attorney subject to the confirmation by the Council. The Metro Attorney serves at the pleasure of the Council and is subject to removal by the Council President with the concurrence of the Council.

(3) Other Offices. The Council may provide by ordinance for the creation of other offices not subordinate to the Chief Operating Officer. The duties and responsibilities of these offices will be more specifically established by ordinance. The Council President appoints all other officers subject to confirmation by the Council. All other officers serve at the pleasure of the Council and are subject to removal by the Council President with the concurrence of the Council.

4) Commissions. The Council may by ordinance create Commissions with duties and responsibilities as specified by the Council. The Council President appoints all Commissioners subject to confirmation by the Council. Commissioners serve at the pleasure of the Council and are subject to removal by the Council President with the concurrence of the Council.

Section 27. Metro Policy Advisory Committee.
(1) Creation and composition. The Metro Policy Advisory Committee (MPAC) is created. The initial members of the MPAC are:

   (a) One member of each of the governing bodies of Washington, Clackamas and Multnomah Counties appointed by the body from which the member is chosen;

   (b) Two members of the governing body of the City of Portland appointed by that governing body;

   (c) One member of the governing body of the second largest city in population in Multnomah County appointed by that governing body;

   (d) One member of the governing body of the largest city in population in Washington County appointed by that governing body;

   (e) One member of the governing body of the largest city in population in Clackamas County appointed by that governing body;

   (f) One member of a governing body of a city with territory in the Metro area in Multnomah County other than either the City of Portland or the second largest city in population in Multnomah County, appointed jointly by the governing bodies of cities with territory in the Metro area in Multnomah County other than the City of Portland or the second largest city in population in Multnomah County;

   (g) One member of a governing body of a city with territory in the Metro area in Washington County other than the city in Washington County with the largest population, appointed jointly by the governing bodies of cities with territory in the Metro area in Washington County other than the city in Washington County with the largest population;

   (h) One member of a governing body of a city with territory in the Metro area in Clackamas County other than the city in Clackamas County with the largest population, appointed jointly by the governing bodies of cities with territory in the Metro area in Clackamas County other than the city in Clackamas County with the largest population;

(i) One member from the governing body of a special district with ter-
     ritory in the Metro area in Multnomah County appointed jointly
     by the governing bodies of special districts with territory in the
     Metro area in Multnomah County;

(j) One member from the governing body of a special district with ter-
     ritory in the Metro area in Washington County appointed jointly
     by the governing bodies of special districts with territory in the
     Metro area in Washington County;

(k) One member from the governing body of a special district with ter-
     ritory in the Metro area in Clackamas County appointed jointly
     by the governing bodies of special districts with territory in the
     Metro area in Clackamas County;

(l) One member of the governing body of Tri-County Metropolitan
     Transportation District of Oregon appointed by the governing body
     of that district; and

(m) Three persons appointed by the Council President and confirmed
     by the council. No person appointed under this part of subsection
     (1) may be an elected officer of or employed by Metro, the state,
     or a city, county or special district. Each person appointed under
     this part of subsection (1) shall reside in the Metro area during the
     person's tenure on the MPAC.

(2) Change of composition. A vote of both a majority of the MPAC members and a majority of all councilors may change the composition of the
MPAC at any time.

(3) Duties. The MPAC shall perform the duties assigned to it by this charter and any other duties the council prescribes.

(4) Bylaws. The MPAC shall adopt bylaws governing the conduct and
record of its meetings and the terms of its members.

Section 28. Metro Office of Citizen Involvement.
(1) Creation and purpose. The Metro office of citizen involvement is created to develop and maintain programs and procedures to aid communication between citizens and the council.

(2) Citizens' committee in office of citizen involvement. The council shall
establish by ordinance (a) a citizens' committee in the office of citizen
involvement and (b) a citizen involvement process. The council shall
appropriate sufficient funds to operate the office and committee.

CHAPTER VI — ELECTIONS AND REAPPORTIONMENT

Section 29. State Law.
Except as this charter or a Metro ordinance provides otherwise, a Metro election shall conform to state law applicable to the election.

Section 30. Elections of Metro Officers.
(1) Generally. Except for certain elections to fill a vacancy in office, the first vote for councilor, council president or auditor occurs at an election held at the same time and places in the Metro area as the statewide primary election that year. If one candidate for a Metro office receives a majority of the votes cast at the primary election for all candidates for that office, that candidate is elected. If no candidate receives a majority of the votes cast at the primary election, the candidates receiving the two largest numbers of votes cast for the office are the only names to appear on the general election ballot that year as candidates for that office. The candidate who receives the largest number of votes cast at the general election for that office is elected.

(2) Nonpartisan offices. All elections of Metro officers are nonpartisan. Election ballots shall list the names of candidates for Metro offices without political party designations.

Section 31. Multiple Candidacies.
No person may be a candidate at a single election for more than one Metro elected office.

Section 32. Reapportionment of Council Districts After Census.
(1) General requirements. Within three months after an official census indicates that the boundaries of council districts deny equal protection of the law, the council shall change the boundaries to accord equal protection of the law and shall assign councilors to the reapportioned districts. As nearly as practicable, all council districts shall be of equal population and each shall be contiguous and geographically compact. The council may by ordinance specify additional criteria for districts that are consistent with this section.

(2) Failure to reapportion. If the council fails to establish council district boundaries as provided by this section, the council president shall establish the boundaries within 60 days.

(3) Redistricting After Year 2000 Census. Within three (3) months after completion of the year 2000 Census, the Council shall establish six (6)

council districts in a manner that accords equal protection of the law. The three (3) councilors serving terms that expire in January 2005 shall each be assigned to one of the six (6) districts and their terms shall continue. Council members will be elected to serve four (4) year terms for the other three (3) districts in the regularly scheduled elections to be held in 2002. For the purpose of Section 33 of this charter, the seven (7) councilors in office in January 2001 shall be deemed to be serving in the districts from which they were elected until January 2003.

Section 33. Recall.
(1) Generally. An elected officer of Metro may be recalled in the manner and with the effect described by the constitution and laws of this state.

(2) Effect of reapportionment. Upon the effective date of a council reapportionment under Section 32 of this charter, a councilor is subject to recall by the voters of the district to which the councilor is assigned and not by the voters of the district of that councilor existing before the reapportionment.

Section 34. Initiative and Referendum.
The voters of Metro reserve to themselves the powers of initiative and referendum. The council may provide for the exercise of those powers in a manner consistent with law.

Section 35. Amendment and Revision of Charter.
The council may refer, and voters of Metro may initiate, amendments to this charter. A proposed charter amendment may embrace only one subject and matters properly connected with it. The council shall provide by ordinance for a procedure to revise this charter.

CHAPTER VII — ORDINANCES

Section 36. Ordaining Clause.
The ordaining clause of an ordinance adopted by the council is: "The Metro Council ordains as follows:." The ordaining clause of an initiated or referred ordinance is: "The People of Metro ordain as follows:."

Section 37. Adoption by Council.
(1) General requirements. The council shall adopt all legislation of Metro by ordinance. Except as this charter otherwise provides, the council may not adopt any ordinance at a meeting unless: (a) the ordinance is introduced at a previous meeting of the council, (b) the title of the ordinance

is included in a written agenda of the meeting at which the ordinance is adopted, (c) the agenda of that meeting is publicized not less than three business days nor more than ten days before the meeting, and (d) copies of the ordinance are available for public inspection at least three business days before that meeting. The text of an ordinance may be amended, but not substantially revised, at the meeting at which it is adopted.

(2) Immediate adoption. The provisions of this section do not apply to an ordinance adopted by unanimous consent of the council and containing findings on the need for immediate adoption.

(3) Vote required. Adoption of an ordinance requires the affirmative votes of (a) seven councilors while the council consists of 13 positions, (b) four councilors after the council consists of seven positions as provided by Section 16(2) of this charter.

Section 38. Endorsement.
The person presiding over the council when an ordinance is adopted shall endorse the ordinance unless the council prescribes a different procedure by general ordinance.

Section 39. Effective Date of Ordinances.
(1) Generally. An ordinance takes effect 90 days after its adoption unless the ordinance states a different effective date. An ordinance may state an earlier effective date if (a) an earlier date is necessary for the health, safety or welfare of the Metro area; (b) the reasons why this is so are stated in an emergency clause of the ordinance; and (c) the ordinance is approved by the affirmative vote of two-thirds of all councilors. An ordinance imposing or changing a tax or charge, changing the boundaries of Metro, or assuming a function may not contain an emergency clause.

(2) Referred ordinances. If the council refers an ordinance to the voters of Metro, the ordinance effective date is the 30th day after its approval by a majority of the voters voting on the measure unless the ordinance specifies a later date. If a referendum petition is filed with the filing officer not later than the 90th day after adoption of an ordinance, the ordinance effective date is suspended. An ordinance is not subject to the referendum after it is effective. An ordinance referred by a referendum petition (a) does not take effect if a majority of the voters voting on the measure reject it and (b) takes effect, unless the ordinance specifies a later date, on the date the results of the election are certified if a majority of the voters voting on the measure approve it.

Section 40. Content of Ordinances.

Each ordinance may embrace only one subject and all matters properly connected with it. The council shall plainly word each ordinance and avoid technical terms as far as practicable.

Section 41. Public Improvements and Special Assessments.

General ordinances govern the procedures for making, altering, vacating or abandoning a public improvement and for fixing, levying and collecting special assessments against real property for public improvements or services. State law governs these procedures to the extent not governed by general ordinances.

CHAPTER VIII — MISCELLANEOUS PROVISIONS

Section 42. Transition Provisions.

All legislation, orders, rules and regulations of the Metropolitan Service District in force when this charter takes effect remain in force after that time to the extent consistent with this charter and until amended or repealed by the council. All rights, claims, causes of action, duties, contracts, and legal and administrative proceedings of the Metropolitan Service District that exist when this charter takes effect continue and are unimpaired by the charter. Each is in the charge of the officer or agency designated by this charter or by its authority to have charge of it. The unexpired terms of elected officers of the Metropolitan Service District continue as provided by this charter. Upon the effective date of this charter, the assets and liabilities of the Metropolitan Service District are the assets and liabilities of Metro.

Section 43. Effective Date.

This charter takes effect January 1, 1993.

Section 44. Severability.

The terms of this charter are severable. If a part of this charter is held invalid, that invalidity does not affect any other part of this charter unless required by the logical relation between the parts.

Section 45. State Legislation.

By adopting this charter the voters of Metro direct the council to seek, and request the Legislative Assembly of this state to enact, any legislation needed to make all parts of this charter operative.

Section 46. Further Transition Provisions.
The amendment to Sections 16(4)(b), 16(5), 18, 20, 23, 26, 27, 28, 32(2) and 39 adopted by the electors of Metro at the November 2000 election take effect on January 6, 2003.[1]

– – – –

Editor's Note: Additional information may be obtained from the Metropolitan Service District, 600 NE Grand Avenue, Portland, Oregon 97232-2736, telephone (503) 797-1700, or directly through their website (http://www.multnomah.lib.or.us/metro/).

Notes

1. Voters approved the Metropolitan Service District's ("Metro's") original home-rule charter in 1992, and amendments to this charter in the November 2000 election. Prior to 1992, Metro's structure and responsibilities were laid out by the Oregon Legislature.

State Government

Edwin Meese III

When the Founding Fathers wrote the Constitution in 1787, the United States only had 13 states. The Founding Fathers believed that more states would want to join the Union in the future. They saw that it would be important for new states to have the same type of government as the original states had. There were 50 states as of 1987, all of which have these characteristics:

- state government is based on a state constitution;
- state has a **republican** form of government;
- state constitution does not contradict the U.S. Constitution; and,
- there are three branches of government — legislative, executive, judicial:
  - separation of powers,
  - **checked and balanced** by each other and by the federal government.

Authority

The states have primary responsibility for many aspects of government. Often the state and federal government work together to provide

Originally published as "State Government," U.S. Government Structure, 1987. Published by the Immigration and Naturalization Service, U.S. Department of Justice, U.S. Government Printing Office, Washington, D.C.

services. Sometimes the state receives federal aid for specific programs. Some services for which the state has primary responsibility include:

- protection of lives and property by maintenance of a police force;
- regulation and improvement of transportation within the state;
- regulation of business within the state; and,
- education.

In providing services the federal and state governments work as partners. Often the federal government provides most of the funding while the state primarily provides distribution though it varies from program to program. Some of these services include:

- health care;
- public assistance for persons in need;
- protection of natural resources; and,
- improvements in living and working conditions.

The Constitution **delegates** any authority not specifically given the federal government in the Constitution to the states. Since the early years of the country, the role of the federal government has grown. Technical advances, such as the telephone, airplane and computer, have brought people and places closer together than they were in 1787. The expanded role of the federal government reflects those changes. State governments, however, serve an important purpose. They are closer to the people than the federal government and can be more responsive to the specific needs of the people in their states.

The Constitution puts one major limitation on state authority. Article VI states that the Constitution, federal laws, and treaties between the U.S. and other countries make up the supreme law of the country. If state or local laws **contradict** any of those, the state or local law can be declared **unconstitutional** by the Supreme Court. Recently, the Supreme Court has used this authority to help guarantee that people's **civil rights** are protected. It has declared laws unconstitutional if they discriminate against people for reason of race, religion, political beliefs or national origin.

Structure

State governments are set up through state constitutions, which usually have four sections. These sections are the:

• preamble;
• bill or declaration of rights;
• outline of the structure of the government; and,
• methods for changing the constitution.

These sections are similar to those in the U.S. Constitution, in form and often in content. The sections usually consist of a:

• **preamble:**
— states the purpose and that the authority of the government comes from the people;
• **bill of rights:**
— includes many of the same rights as in the U.S. Constitution's Bill of Rights;
— sometimes additional rights, such as the right to work, are included;
• **structure section:**
— sets up the three separate branches: the executive, judicial and legislative; and,
• **methods of change:**
— states the procedure for amending or redrafting the constitution.

State constitutions sometimes set up procedures or guarantee rights not mentioned in the U.S. Constitution. Some states guarantee that workers will not lose their jobs if they do not belong to a union or have a special statement on equal rights for women. States also must establish procedures for local governments within the state, such as the process for granting a city **charter**. Some states provide their citizens with opportunities for **direct democracy**. The federal government could not easily do this because the number of people and size of the country would make it difficult to implement. The states, being smaller and more able to respond to the local needs than the federal government, often provide one or more types of direct democracy. The major types are the

- **initiative**;
- **referendum**; and,
- **recall**.

The *initiative* usually is used to pass laws or amend the state constitution. A group of concerned citizens draws up a **petition**. The petition states the problem and a solution. If the required number of people signs the petition, the issue is put on the ballot and the people vote on it. At least 50 percent (or half) must vote in favor of the issue for it to pass.

Referenda work in a slightly different way. There are three different types: the *compulsory referendum*, *optional referendum*, and *petition* or *protest referendum*. Some states require that certain issues, such as amendments to the state constitution, be submitted to a popular vote. This is the *compulsory referendum*. State legislatures sometimes use the *optional referendum* to settle a highly **controversial** issue. When the citizens vote, that tells the legislature what the people believe should be done about the issue. The *protest referendum* gives citizens who are not pleased with a law a chance to overturn the law. A certain number of citizens must sign a petition to submit the issue to popular vote. The outcome of the vote determines whether the law remains or is overturned.

The *recall* provides citizens with a chance to remove an official from office. Sometimes judges and appointed officials are **exempt** from recall. In other states the citizens can vote to remove any public official who they believe is not serving the best interests of the government and people. As with the initiative and the protest referendum, a certain number of people must sign a petition to put the recall issue on the ballot. These examples of direct democracy — the initiative, referendum, and recall — provide citizens with the opportunity to be involved in issues which they consider very important.

State and local government, like the federal government, is based on the principle of **representative democracy**. Though many states provide opportunities for direct democracy, most governing is done by elected representatives. One of the most important functions of the state constitution is to establish the structure of the state government. All state governments have three branches — the executive, legislative and judicial. Details of government structure vary between states, but the basic structure is similar. For information about a specific state, contact its *League of Women Voters*, the *National Municipal League*, or another civic group.

EXECUTIVE BRANCH

The head of every state government is the governor. The qualifications, terms of office and powers of the governor are listed below:

- Qualifications vary, but candidates for governor of a state usually must be qualified voters, citizens of the U.S., of a certain age (usually more than 30) and have lived in the state a certain period of time (often five years).
- The term of office varies, usually either two or four years.
  — In some states, there is a limit to the number of times the governor can serve.
- The powers of the governor are similar in all states:
  — Advise the state legislature on the laws needed;
  — Call special sessions of the state legislature;
  — Serve as head of the state's **National Guard**;
  — Pardon or decrease sentences of people convicted in state courts, when appropriate.
- If the governor dies or is unable to serve, the **lieutenant governor**, whose position is similar to that of the Vice President, becomes governor.

The governor has a group of advisers, similar to the President's Cabinet, who perform special services for the state. In some states, voters elect these officials, and in others the governor appoints them. Some of these are:

- Secretary of State, who keeps official records and publishes state laws;
- Attorney General, who represents the state in court;
- Treasurer, who receives tax money and pays bills for the state from that money;
- Auditor or Comptroller, who keeps track of the financial matters in the state; and,
- various commissioners, who are concerned with such issues as labor, banking, public utilities, and health.

The governor and his/her advisers not only carry out the laws passed by the state legislature, but propose new laws. Governors often are elected on a specific **platform** and try to get the legislature to pass their new proposals.

LEGISLATIVE BRANCH

Each state has a legislature similar to the federal government. Forty-nine of the states have **bicameral legislatures**, meaning they have two houses, similar to the federal government. (Nebraska is the exception — it only has one house.) The two houses usually are called the **house of representatives** and the **senate**. Each state sets its own requirements and structure for its legislature.

- The purposes of all state legislatures are:
  — to make laws about state matters, and

  — to represent the interests of its citizens.
- The term of office varies from state to state. Usually, a term is four years in the senate and two years in the house of representatives. However, it can be four years or two years in each.
- Distribution of representatives differs by state.
  — Some states have a set number of representatives for a set geographic area, such as one representative for every 10 square miles.
  — Some states have representation based on population, such as a representative for every 20,000 people.
  — In some states, representatives are *at-large*, and all voters help elect all representatives.
- The procedure for making laws is similar to the procedure followed in the federal government.

JUDICIAL BRANCH

The state courts have a **hierarchy** which is similar to the federal system. The structure, from lowest to highest, is:

- justice of the peace, municipal, county or special courts;
- district, superior, circuit or common pleas courts;
- intermediate appellate courts (not in all states); and,
- state supreme court.

There are two kinds of cases: **civil** and **criminal**. Judges, who usually are elected, **preside** over all cases. Most cases also have **juries**. Trial by jury is guaranteed by the U.S. Constitution in most cases. Juries consist of citizens who listen to the lawyers argue both sides of the case and to the judge's instructions. Then the jury decides, by a vote, whether the accused person is guilty or innocent. The jury also may make recommendations about punishment of those found guilty, but the judge has the final authority on punishment and **sentencing**.

State courts only hear cases that involve state or local laws, so they have somewhat different duties than federal courts. Some of their duties are:

- to explain state laws;
- to tell how state laws apply;
- to settle disagreements between citizens in a state;
- to decide guilt or innocence of breaking a state law; and,
- to decide if state laws are unconstitutional.

Responsibilities

Citizens and state governments have important responsibilities to each other. Since states have fewer people than the country, citizens have more personal contact with their state governments. Usually it is easier for the citizen and state to remind each other of their responsibilities. Citizens in the state have a responsibility to:

- obey state laws;
- pay their state taxes;
- vote in all state elections; and,
- be informed and participating citizens.

States have responsibilities to their citizens to:

- protect the lives and property of people in the state;
- provide certain basic services, such as education; and,
- provide government and justice according to state and federal laws.

These requirements—authority, structure (legislative, executive, and judicial), and responsibilities—are embodied in every state's charter, or constitution. Also, most states provide citizens with one or more avenues

of direct democracy. That is, constitutional provisions and legal requirements for a citizen-initiated initiative, referendum, or recall. (Last paragraph added by Editor).

– – – –

Editor's Note: A copy of this entire book, *U.S. Government Structure* (1987), may be
obtained from the U.S. Government Printing Office, P.O. Box 371954, Pittsburgh, Pennsylvania 15250-7954, or may be ordered over the internet from GPO's online bookstore (http://bookstore.gpo.gov). Another excellent book, *Our American Government*
(1993), is also available from this same source.

MODEL STATE GOVERNMENT CHARTER
Frank P. Grad

The Model State Constitution

PREAMBLE

We, the people of the state of _____, recognizing the rights and duties of this state as a part of the federal system of government, reaffirm our adherence to the Constitution of the United States of America; and in order to assure the state government power to act for the good order of the state and the liberty, health, safety and welfare of the people, we do ordain and establish this constitution.

ARTICLE I
Bill of Rights

Section 1.01. *Freedom of Religion, Speech, Press, Assembly and Petition.* No law shall be enacted respecting an establishment of religion, or prohibiting the free exercise thereof, or abridging the freedom of speech or of the press, or the right of the people peaceably to assemble and to petition the government for a redress of grievances.

Section 1.02. *Due Process and Equal Protection.* No person shall be deprived of life, liberty or property without due process of law, nor be denied the equal protection of the laws, nor be denied the enjoyment of his civil rights or be discriminated against in the exercise thereof because of race, national origin, religion or ancestry.

Section 1.03. *Searches and Seizures and Interceptions.*

(a) The right of the people to be secure in their persons, houses, papers and effects against unreasonable searches and seizures shall not be violated, and no warrants shall issue, but upon probable cause, supported by oath or affirmation, and particularly describing the place to be searched and the persons or things to be seized.

(b) The right of the people to be secure against unreasonable interception of telephone, telegraph and other electronic means of communication, and against unreasonable interception of oral and other communications by electric or electronic methods, shall not be violated, and no orders and warrants for such interceptions shall issue but upon probable cause supported by oath or affirmation that evidence of crime may be thus obtained, and particularly identifying the means of communication and the person or persons whose communications are to be intercepted.

(c) Evidence obtained in violation of this section shall not be admissible in any court against any person.

Section 1.04. *Self-Incrimination.* No person shall be compelled to give testimony which might tend to incriminate him.

Section 1.05. *Writ of Habeas Corpus.* The privilege of the writ of habeas corpus shall not be suspended unless when in cases of rebellion or invasion the public safety may require it.

Section 1.06. *Rights of Accused Persons.*

(a) In all criminal prosecutions the accused shall enjoy the right to a speedy and public trial, to be informed of the nature and cause of the accusation, to be confronted with the witnesses against him, to have compulsory process for obtaining witnesses in his favor, to have the assistance of counsel for his defense, and to the assignment of counsel to represent him at every stage of the proceedings unless he elects to proceed without counsel or is able to obtain counsel. In prosecutions for felony, the accused shall also enjoy the right of trial by an impartial jury of the county [or other appropriate political subdivision of the state] wherein the crime shall have been committed, or of another county, if a change of venue has been granted.

(b) All persons shall, before conviction, be bailable by sufficient sureties, but bail may be denied to persons charged with capital offenses or offenses punishable by life imprisonment, giving due weight to the evidence and to the nature and circumstances of the event. Excessive bail shall not be required, nor excessive fines imposed, nor cruel or unusual punishment inflicted.

(c) No person shall be twice put in jeopardy for the same offense.

Section 1.07. *Political Tests for Public Office.* No oath, declaration or political test shall be required for any public office or employment other than the following oath or affirmation: "I do solemnly swear [or affirm] that I will support and defend the Constitution of the United States and the constitution of the state of _____ and that I will faithfully discharge the duties of the office of _____ to the best of my ability."

ARTICLE II

Powers of the State

Section 2.01. *Powers of Government.* The enumeration in this constitution of specified powers and functions shall be construed neither as a grant nor as a limitation of the powers of state government but the state government shall have all of the powers not denied by this constitution or by or under the Constitution of the United States.

ARTICLE III

Suffrage and Elections

Section 3.01. *Qualifications for Voting.* Every citizen of the age of _____ years and a resident of the state for three months shall have the right to vote in the election of all officers that may be elected by the people and upon all questions that may be submitted to the voters; but the legislature may by law establish: (1) Minimum periods of local residence not exceeding three months, (2) reasonable requirements to determine literacy in English or in another language predominantly used in the classrooms of any public or private school accredited by any state or territory of the United States, the District of Columbia, or the Commonwealth of Puerto Rico, and (3) disqualifications for voting for mental incompetency or conviction of felony.

Section 3.02. *Legislature to Prescribe for Exercise of Suffrage.* The legislature shall by law define residence for voting purposes, insure secrecy in voting and provide for the registration of voters, absentee voting, the administration of elections and the nomination of candidates.

ARTICLE IV

The Legislature

Section 4.01. *Legislative Power.* The legislative power of the state shall be vested in the legislature.

Section 4.02. *Composition of the Legislature.* The legislature shall be composed of a single chamber consisting of one member to represent each legislative district. The number of members shall be prescribed by law but shall not be less than _____ nor exceed _____. Each member of the legislature shall be a qualified voter of the state and shall be at least _____ years of age.

> BICAMERAL ALTERNATIVE: Section 4.02. *Composition of the Legislature.* The legislature shall be composed of a senate and an assembly. The number of members of each house of the legislature shall be prescribed by law but the number of assemblymen shall not be less than _____ nor exceed _____, and the number of senators shall not exceed one-third, as near as may be, the number of assemblymen. Each assemblyman shall represent one assembly district and each senator shall represent one senate district. Each member of the legislature shall be a qualified voter of the state and shall be at least _____ years of age.

Section 4.03. *Election and Term of Members.* The members of the legislature shall be elected by the qualified voters of the state for a term of two years.

> BICAMERAL ALTERNATIVE: Section 4.03. *Election and Terms of Members.* Assemblymen shall be elected by the qualified voters of the state for a term of two years and senators for a term of six years. One-third of the senators shall be elected every two years.

Section 4.04. *Legislative Districts.*

(a) For the purpose of electing members of the legislature, the state shall be divided into as many districts as there shall be members of the legislature. Each district shall consist of compact and contiguous territory. All districts shall be so nearly equal in population that the population of the largest district shall not exceed that of the smallest district by more than _____ per cent. In determining the population of each district, inmates of such public or private institutions as prisons or other places of correction, hospitals for the insane or other institutions housing persons who are disqualified from voting by law shall not be counted.

(b) Immediately following each decennial census, the governor shall appoint a board of _____ qualified voters to make recommendations within ninety days of their appointment concerning the redistricting of the state. The governor shall publish the recommendations of the board when received. The governor shall promulgate a redistricting plan within ninety to one hundred and twenty days after appointment of the board, whether or not it has made its recommendations. The governor shall accompany his plan with a message explaining his reasons for any changes from the recommendations of the board. The governor's redistricting plan shall be published in the manner provided for acts of the legislature and shall have the force of law upon such publication. Upon the application of any qualified voter, the supreme court, in the exercise of original, exclusive and final jurisdiction, shall review the governor's redistricting plan and shall have jurisdiction to make orders to amend the plan to comply with the requirements of this constitution or, if the governor has failed to promulgate a redistricting plan within the time provided, to make one or more orders establishing such a plan.

BICAMERAL ALTERNATIVE: Section 4.04. *Legislative Districts.*

(a) For the purpose of electing members of the assembly, the state shall be divided into as many districts as there shall be members of the assembly. Each district shall consist of compact and contiguous territory. All districts shall be so nearly equal in population that the district with the greatest population shall not exceed the district with the least population by more than _____ per cent. In determining the population of each district, inmates of such public or private institutions as prisons or other places of correction, hospitals for the insane or other institutions housing persons who are disqualified from voting by law shall not be counted.

(b) For the purpose of electing members of the senate, the state shall be divided into as many districts as there shall be members of the senate. Each senate district shall consist of a compact and contiguous territory. All districts shall be so nearly equal in population that the district with the greatest population shall not exceed the district with the least population by more than _____ per cent. In determining the population of each district, inmates of such public or private institutions as prisons or other places of correction, hospitals for the insane or other institutions housing persons who are disqualified from voting by law shall not be counted.

(c) Immediately following each decennial census, the governor shall appoint a board of _____ qualified voters to make recommendations within ninety days of their appointment concerning the redistricting of the state. The governor shall publish the recommendations of the board when received. The governor shall promulgate a redistricting plan within ninety to one hundred and twenty days after appointment of the board, whether or not it has made its recommendations. The governor shall accompany his plan with a message explaining his reasons for any changes from the recommendations of the board. The governor's redistricting plan shall be published in the manner provided for acts of the legislature and shall have the force of law upon such publication. Upon the application of any qualified voter, the supreme court, in the exercise of original, exclusive and final jurisdiction, shall review the governor's redistricting plan and shall have jurisdiction to make orders to amend the plan to comply with the requirements of this constitution or, if the governor has failed to promulgate a redistricting plan within the time provided, to make one or more orders establishing such a plan.

Section 4.05. *Time of Election.* Members of the legislature shall be elected at the regular election in each odd-numbered year.

Section 4.06. *Vacancies.* When a vacancy occurs in the legislature it shall be filled as provided by law.

Section 4.07. *Compensation of Members.* The members of the legislature shall receive an annual salary and such allowances as may be prescribed by law but any increase or decrease in the amount thereof shall not apply to the legislature which enacted the same.

Section 4.08. *Sessions.* The legislature shall be a continuous body during the term for which its members are elected. It shall meet in regular sessions annually as provided by law. It may be convened at other times by the governor or, at the written request of a majority of the members, by the presiding officer of the legislature.

> BICAMERAL ALTERNATIVE: Section 4.08. *Sessions.* The legislature shall be a continuous body during the term for which members of the assembly are elected. The legislature shall meet in regular sessions annually as provided by law. It may be convened at other times by the governor or, at the written request of a majority of the members of each house, by the presiding officers of both houses.

Section 4.09. *Organization and Procedure.* The legislature shall be the final judge of the election and qualifications of its members and may by law vest in the courts the trial and determination of contested elections of members. It shall choose its presiding officer from among its members and it shall employ a secretary to serve for an indefinite term. It shall determine its rules of procedure; it may compel the attendance of absent members, discipline its members and, with the concurrence of two-thirds of all the members, expel a member, and it shall have power to compel the attendance and testimony of witnesses and the production of books and papers either before the legislature as a whole or before any committee thereof. The secretary of the legislature shall be its chief fiscal, administrative and personnel officer and shall perform such duties as the legislature may prescribe.

BICAMERAL ALTERNATIVE: Section 4.09. *Organization and Procedure.* Each house of the legislature shall be the final judge of the election and qualifications of its members and the legislature may by law vest in the courts the trial and determination of contested elections of members. Each house of the legislature shall choose its presiding officer from among its members and it shall employ a secretary to serve for an indefinite term, and each house shall determine its rules of procedure; it may compel the attendance of absent members, discipline its members and, with the concurrence of two-thirds of all the members, expel a member, and it shall have power to compel the attendance and testimony of witnesses and the production of books and papers either before such house of the legislature as a whole or before any committee thereof. The secretary of each house of the legislature shall be its chief fiscal, administrative and personnel officer and shall perform such duties as each such house of the legislature may prescribe.

Section 4.10. *Legislative Immunity.* For any speech or debate in the legislature, the members shall not be questioned in any other place.

Section 4.11. *Special Legislation.* The legislature shall pass no special or local act when a general act is or can be made applicable, and whether a general act is or can be made applicable shall be a matter for judicial determination.

Section 4.12. *Transaction of Business.* A majority of all the members of the legislature shall constitute a quorum to do business but a smaller number may adjourn from day to day and compel the attendance of absent members. The legislature shall keep a journal of its proceedings which shall be published from day to day. The legislature shall prescribe the methods of voting on legislative matters but a record vote, with the yeas and nays entered in the journal, shall be taken on any question on the demand of one-fifth of the members present.

> BICAMERAL ALTERNATIVE: Section 4.12. *Transaction of Business.* Refer to "each house of the legislature" instead of "the legislature" wherever appropriate.

Section 4.13. *Committees.* The legislature may establish such committees as it may deem necessary for the conduct of its business. When a committee to which a bill has been assigned has not reported on it, one-third of all the members of the legislature shall have power to relieve it of further consideration. Adequate public notice of all committee hearings, with a clear statement of all subjects to be considered at each hearing, shall be published in advance.

> BICAMERAL ALTERNATIVE: Section 4.13. *Committees.* Refer to "each house of the legislature" instead of "the legislature" wherever appropriate.

Section 4.14. *Bills; Single Subject.* The legislature shall enact no law except by bill and every bill except bills for appropriations and bills for the codification, revision or rearrangement of existing laws shall be confined to one subject. All appropriation bills shall be limited to the subject of appropriations. Legislature compliance with the requirements of this section is a constitutional responsibility not subject to judicial review.

Section 4.15. *Passage of Bills.* No bill shall become a law unless its has been printed and upon the desks of the members in final form at least three days prior to final passage and the majority of all the members has assented to it. The yeas and nays on final passage shall be entered in the journal. The legislature shall provide for the publication of all acts and no act shall become effective until published as provided by law.

> BICAMERAL ALTERNATIVE: Section 4.15. *Passage of Bills.* Refer to "each house of the legislature" instead of "the legislature" wherever appropriate.

Section 4.16. *Action by the Governor.*

(a) When a bill has passed the legislature, it shall be presented to the governor and, if the legislature is in session, it shall become law if the governor either signs or fails to veto it within fifteen days of presentation. If the legislature is in recess or, if the session of the legislature has expired during such fifteen-day period, it shall become law if he signs it within thirty days after such adjournment or expiration. If the governor does not approve a bill, he shall veto it and return it to the legislature either within fifteen days of presentation if the legislature is in session or upon the reconvening of the legislature from its recess. Any bill so returned by the governor shall be reconsidered by the legislature and, if upon reconsideration two-thirds of all the members shall agree to pass the bill, it shall become law.

(b) The governor may strike out or reduce items in appropriation bills passed by the legislature and the procedure in such cases shall be the same as in case of the disapproval of an entire bill by the governor.

> BICAMERAL ALTERNATIVE: Section 4.16. *Action by the Governor.* Refer to "each house of the legislature" instead of "the legislature" wherever appropriate.

Section 4.17. *Post-Audit.* The legislature shall appoint an auditor to serve at its pleasure. The auditor shall conduct post-audits as prescribed by law and shall report to the legislature and to the governor.

> BICAMERAL ALTERNATIVE: Section 4.17. *Post-Audit.* The legislature shall, by joint resolution, appoint … .

Section 4.18. *Impeachment.* The legislature may impeach the governor, the heads of principal departments, judicial officers and such other officers of the state as may be made subject to impeachment by law, by a two-thirds vote of all the members, and shall provide by law procedures for the trial and removal from office, after conviction, of officers so impeached. No officer shall be convicted on impeachment by a vote of less than two-thirds of the members of the tribunal hearing the charges.

> BICAMERAL ALTERNATIVE: Section 4.18. *Impeachment.* Refer to "by a two-thirds vote of all the members of each house."

ARTICLE V
The Executive

Section 5.01. *Executive Power.* The executive power of the state shall be vested in a governor.

Section 5.02. *Election and Qualifications of Governor.* The governor shall be elected, at the regular election every other odd-numbered year, by the direct vote of the people, for a term of four years beginning on the first day of [December] [January] next following his election. Any qualified voter of the state who is at least _____ years of age shall be eligible to the office of governor.

Section 5.03. *Governor's Messages to the Legislature.* The governor shall, at the beginning of each session, and may, at other times, give to the legislature information as to the affairs of the state and recommend measures he considers necessary or desirable.

Section 5.04. *Executive and Administrative Powers.*

(a) The governor shall be responsible for the faithful execution of the laws. He may, by appropriate action or proceeding brought in the name of the state, enforce compliance with any constitutional or legislative mandate, or restrain violation of any constitutional or legislative power, duty or right by an officer, department or agency of the state or any of its civil divisions. This authority shall not authorize any action or proceeding against the legislature.

(b) The governor shall commission all officers of the state. He may at any time require information, in writing or otherwise, from the officers of any administrative department, office or agency upon any subject relating to the respective offices. He shall be commander-in-chief of the armed forces of the state, except when they shall be called into the service of the United States, and may call them out to execute the laws, to preserve order, to suppress insurrection or to repel invasion.

Section 5.05. *Executive Clemency.* The governor shall have power to grant reprieves, commutations and pardons, after conviction, for all offenses and may delegate such powers, subject to such procedures as may be prescribed by law.

Section 5.06. *Administrative Departments.* All executive and administrative offices, agencies and instrumentalities of the state government, and their respective functions, powers and duties, shall be allocated by law among and within not more than twenty principal departments so as to group them as far as practicable according to major purposes. Regulatory, quasi-judicial and temporary agencies established by law may, but need not, be allocated within a principal department. The legislature shall by law prescribe the functions, powers and duties of the principal departments and of all other agencies of the state and may from time to time reallocate offices, agencies and instrumentalities among the principal departments, may increase, modify, diminish or change their functions, powers and duties and may assign new functions, powers and duties to them; but the governor may make such changes in the allocation of offices, agencies and instrumentalities, and in the allocation of such functions, powers and duties, as he considers necessary for efficient administration. If such changes affect existing law, they shall be set forth in executive orders, which shall be submitted to the legislature while it is in session, and shall become effective, and shall have the force of law, sixty days after submission, or at the close of the session, whichever is sooner, unless specifically modified or disapproved by a resolution concurred in by a majority of all the members.

> BICAMERAL ALTERNATIVE: Section 5.06. *Administrative Departments.* Change the last phrase to read "majority of all the members of each house."

Section 5.07. *Executive Officers; Appointment.* The governor shall appoint and may remove the heads of all administrative departments. All other officers in the administrative service of the state shall be appointed and may be removed as provided by law.

Section 5.08. *Succession to Governorship.*

(a) If the governor-elect fails to assume office for any reason, the presiding officer of the legislature shall serve as acting governor until the governor-elect qualifies and assumes office or, if the governor-elect does not assume office within six months, until the unexpired term has been filled by special election and the newly elected governor has qualified. If, at the time the presiding officer of the legislature is to assume the acting governorship, the legislature has not yet organized and elected a presiding officer, the outgoing governor shall hold over until the presiding officer of the legislature is elected.

(b) When the governor is unable to discharge the duties of his office by reason of impeachment or other disability, including but not limited to physical or mental disability, or when the duties of the office are not being discharged by reason of his continuous absence, the presiding officer of the legislature shall serve as acting governor until the governor's disability or absence terminates. If the governor's disability or absence does not terminate within six months, the office of the governor shall be vacant.

(c) When, for any reason, a vacancy occurs in the office of the governor, the unexpired term shall be filled by special election except when such unexpired term is less than one year, in which event the presiding officer of the legislature shall succeed to the office for the remainder of the term. When a vacancy in the office of the governor is filled by special election, the presiding officer of the legislature shall serve as acting governor from the occurrence of the vacancy until the newly elected governor has qualified. When the presiding officer of the legislature succeeds to the office of governor, he shall have the title, powers, duties and emoluments of that office and, when he serves as acting governor, he shall have the powers and duties thereof and shall receive such compensation as the legislature shall provide by law.

(d) The legislature shall provide by law for special elections to fill vacancies in the office of the governor.

(e) The supreme court shall have original, exclusive and final jurisdiction to determine absence and disability of the governor or governor-elect and to determine the existence of a vacancy in the office of governor and all questions concerning succession to the office or to its powers and duties.

> BICAMERAL ALTERNATIVE: Section 5.08. *Succession to Governorship.* For "presiding officer of the legislature" substitute "presiding officer of the senate."

ARTICLE VI
The Judiciary

Section 6.01. *Judicial Power.* The judicial power of the state shall be vested in a unified judicial system, which shall include a supreme court, an appellate court and a general court, and which shall also include such inferior courts of limited jurisdiction as may from time to time be established by law. All courts except the supreme court may be divided into geographical departments or districts as provided by law and into functional divisions and subdivisions as provided by law or by judicial rules not inconsistent with law.

Section 6.02. *Supreme Court.* The supreme court shall be the highest court of the state and shall consist of a chief judge and _____ associate judges.

Section 6.03. *Jurisdiction of Courts.* The supreme court shall have appellate jurisdiction in all cases arising under this constitution and the Constitution of the United States and in all other cases as provided by law. It shall also have original jurisdiction in cases arising under subsections

4.04(b) and 5.08(e) of this constitution and in all other cases as provided by law. All other courts of the state shall have original and appellate jurisdiction as provided by law, which jurisdiction shall be uniform in all geographical departments or districts of the same court. The jurisdiction of functional divisions and subdivisions shall be as provided by law or by judicial rules not inconsistent with law.

Section 6.04. *Appointment of Judges; Qualifications; Tenure; Retirement; Removal.*

(a) The governor, with the advice and consent of the legislature, shall appoint the chief judges and associate judges of the supreme, appellate and general courts. The governor shall give ten days' public notice before sending a judicial nomination to the legislature or before making an interim appointment when the legislature is not in session.

> ALTERNATIVE: Subsection 6.04(a). *Nomination by Nominating Commission.* The governor shall fill a vacancy in the offices of the chief judges and associate judges of the supreme, appellate and general courts from a list of nominees presented to him by the appropriate judicial nominating commission. If the governor fails to make an appointment within sixty days from the day the list is presented, the appointment shall be made by the chief judge or by the acting chief judge from the same list. There shall be a judicial nominating commission for the supreme court and one commission for the nomination of judges for the court sitting in each geographical department or district of the appellate court. Each judicial nominating commission shall consist of seven members, one of whom shall be the chief judge of the supreme court, who shall act as chairman. The members of the bar of the state in the geographical area for which the court or the department or district of the court sits shall elect three of their number to be members of such a commission, and the governor shall appoint three citizens, not members of the bar, from among the residents of the same geographical area. The terms of office and the compensation for members of a judicial nominating commission shall be as provided by law. No member of a judicial nominating commission except the chief judge shall hold any other public office or office in any political party or organization, and no member of such a commission shall be eligible for appointment to a state judicial office so long as he is a member of such a commission and for [five] [three] [two] years thereafter.

(b) No person shall be eligible for judicial office in the supreme court, appellate court and general court unless he has been admitted to practice law before the supreme court for at least _____ years. No person who holds judicial office in the supreme court, appellate court or general court shall hold any other paid office, position of profit or employment under the state, its civil divisions or the United States. Any judge of the supreme court, appellate court or general court who becomes a candidate for an elective office shall thereby forfeit his judicial office.

(c) The judges of the supreme court, appellate court and general court shall hold their offices for initial terms of seven years and upon reappointment shall hold their offices during good behavior. They shall be retired upon attaining the age of seventy years and may be pensioned as may be provided by law. The chief judge of the supreme court may from time to time appoint retired judges to such special assignments as may be provided by the rules of the supreme court.

(d) The judges of the supreme court, appellate court and general court shall be subject to impeachment and any such judge impeached shall not exercise his office until acquitted. The supreme court may also remove judges of the appellate and general courts for such cause and in such manner as may be provided by law.

(e) The legislature shall provide by law for the appointment of judges of the inferior courts and for their qualifications, tenure, retirement and removal.

(f) The judges of the courts of this state shall receive such salaries as may be provided by law, which shall not be diminished during their term of office.

Section 6.05. *Administration.* The chief judge of the supreme court shall be the administrative head of the unified judicial system. He may assign judges from one geographical department or functional division of a court to another department or division of that court and he may assign judges for temporary service from one court to another. The chief judge shall, with the approval of the supreme court, appoint an administrative director to serve at his pleasure and to supervise the administrative operation of the judicial system.

Section 6.06. *Financing.* The chief judge shall submit an annual consolidated budget for the entire unified judicial system and the total cost of the system shall be paid by the state. The legislature may provide by law for the reimbursement to the state of appropriate portions of such cost by political subdivisions.

Section 6.07. *Rule-making Power.* The supreme court shall make and promulgate rules governing the administration of all courts. It shall make and promulgate rules governing practice and procedure in civil and criminal cases in all courts. These rules may be changed by the legislature by a two-thirds vote of all the members.

Article VII
Finance

Section 7.01. *State Debt.* No debt shall be contracted by or on behalf of this state unless such debt shall be authorized by law for projects or objects distinctly specified therein.

Section 7.02. *The Budget.* The governor shall submit to the legislature, at a time fixed by law, a budget estimate for the next fiscal year setting forth all proposed expenditures and anticipated income of all departments and agencies of the state, as well as a general appropriation bill to authorize the proposed expenditures and a bill or bills covering recommendations in the budget for new or additional revenues.

Section 7.03. *Expenditure of Money.*

(a) No money shall be withdrawn from the treasury except in accordance with appropriations made by law, nor shall any obligation for the payment of money be incurred except as authorized by law. The appropriation for each department, office or agency of the state, for which appropriation is made, shall be for a specific sum of money and no appropriation shall allocate to any object the proceeds of any particular tax or fund or a part or percentage thereof, except when required by the federal government for participation in federal programs.

(b) All state and local expenditures, including salaries paid by the legislative, executive and judicial branches of government, shall be matters of public record.

Article VIII
Local Government

Section 8.01. *Organization of Local Government.* The legislature shall provide by general law for the government of counties, cities and other civil divisions and for methods and procedures of incorporating, merging, consolidating and dissolving such civil divisions and of altering their boundaries, including provisions:

(1) For such classification of civil divisions as may be necessary, on the basis of population or on any other reasonable basis related to the purpose of the classification;

(2) For optional plans of municipal organization and government so as to enable a county, city or other civil division to adopt or abandon an authorized optional charter by a majority vote of the qualified voters voting thereon;

(3) For the adoption or amendment of charters by any county or city for its own government, by a majority vote of the qualified voters of the city or county voting thereon, for methods and procedures for the selection of charter commissions, and for framing, publishing, disseminating and adopting such charters or charter amendments and for meeting the expenses connected therewith.

ALTERNATIVE PARAGRAPH: Section 8.01(3). *Self-Executing Home Rule Powers.* For the adoption or amendment of charters by any county or city, in accordance with the provisions of section 8.02 concerning home rule for local units.

Section 8.02. *Powers of Counties and Cities.* A county or city may exercise any legislative power or perform any function which is not denied to it by its charter, is not denied to counties or cities generally, or to counties or cities of its class, and is within such limitations as the legislature may establish by general law. This grant of home rule powers shall not include the power to enact private or civil law governing civil relationships except as incident to an exercise of an independent county or city power, nor shall it include power to define and provide for the punishment of a felony.

ALTERNATIVE PROVISIONS FOR SELF-EXECUTING HOME RULE POWERS: Section 8.02. *Home Rule for Local Units.*

(a) Any county or city may adopt or amend a charter for its own government, subject to such regulations as are provided in this constitution and may be provided by general law. The legislature shall provide one or more optional procedures for nonpartisan election of five, seven or nine charter commissioners and for framing, publishing and adopting a charter or charter amendments.

(b) Upon resolution approved by a majority of the members of the legislative authority of the county or city or upon petition of ten per cent of the qualified voters, the officer or agency responsible for certifying public questions shall submit to the people at the next regular election not less than sixty days thereafter, or at a special election if authorized by law, the question "Shall a commission be chosen to frame a charter or charter amendments for the county [or city] of _____?" An affirmative vote of a majority of the qualified voters voting on the question shall authorize the creation of the commission.

(c) A petition to have a charter commission may include the names of five, seven or nine commissioners, to be listed at the end of the question when it is voted on, so that an affirmative vote on the question is a vote to elect the persons named in the petition. Otherwise, the petition or resolution shall designate an optional election procedure provided by law.

(d) Any proposed charter or charter amendments shall be published by the commission, distributed to the qualified voters and submitted to them at the next regular or special election not less than thirty days after publication. The procedure for publication and submission shall be as provided by law or by resolution of the charter commission not inconsistent with law. The legislative authority of the county or city shall, on request of the charter commission, appropriate money to provide for the reasonable expenses of the commission and for the publication, distribution and submission of its proposals.

(e) A charter or charter amendments shall become effective if approved by a majority vote of the qualified voters voting thereon. A charter may provide for direct submission of future charter revisions or amendments by petition or by resolution of the local legislature authority.

Section 8.03. *Powers of Local Units.* Counties shall have such powers as shall be provided by general or optional law. Any city or other civil division may, by agreement, subject to a local referendum and the approval of a majority of the qualified voters voting any of its functions or powers and may revoke the transfer of any such function or power, under regulations provided by general law; and any county may, in like manner, transfer to another county or to a city within its boundaries or adjacent thereto any of its functions or powers and may revoke the transfer of any such function or power.

Section 8.04. *County Government.* Any county charter shall provide the form of government of the county and shall determine which of its officers shall be elected and the manner of their election. It shall provide for the exercise of all powers vested in, and the performance of all duties imposed upon, counties and county officers by law. Such charter may provide for the concurrent or exclusive exercise by the county, in all or in part of its area, of all or of any designated powers vested by the constitution or laws of this state in cities and other civil divisions; it may provide for the succession by the county to the rights, properties and obligations of cities and other civil divisions therein incident to the powers so vested in the county, and for the division of the county into districts for purposes of administration or of taxation or of both. No provision of any charter or amendment vesting in the county any powers of a city or other civil division shall become effective unless it shall have been approved by a majority of those voting thereon (1) in the county, (2) in any city containing more than twenty-five per cent of the total population of the county, and (3) in the county outside of such city or cities.

Section 8.05. *City Government.* Except as provided in sections 8.03 and 8.04, each city is hereby granted full power and authority to pass laws and ordinances relating to its local affairs, property and government; and no enumeration of powers in this constitution shall be deemed to limit or restrict the general grant of authority hereby conferred; but this grant of authority shall not be deemed to limit or restrict the power of the legislature to enact laws of statewide concern uniformly applicable to every city.

> FURTHER ALTERNATIVE: A further alternative is possible by combining parts of the basic text of this article and parts of the foregoing alternative. If the self-executing alternative section 8.02 is preferred but not the formulation of home rule powers in alternative sections 8.03, 8.04 and 8.05, the following combination of sections will combine the self-executing feature and the power formulation included in the basic text:
>
> Section 8.01. *Organization of Local Government*, with alternative paragraph (3).
>
> Alternative Section 8.02. *Home Rule for Local Units.*
>
> Section 8.02, renumbered 8.03. *Powers of Counties and Cities.*

ARTICLE IX
Public Education

Section 9.01. *Free Public Schools; Support of Higher Education.* The legislature shall provide for the maintenance and support of a system of free public schools open to all children in the state and shall establish, organize and support such other public educational institutions, including public institutions of higher learning, as may be desirable.

ARTICLE X
Civil Service

Section 10.01. *Merit System.* The legislature shall provide for the establishment and administration of a system of personnel administration in the civil service of the state and its civil divisions. Appointments and promotions shall be based on merit and fitness, demonstrated by examination or by other evidence of competence.

ARTICLE XI
Intergovernmental Relations

Section 11.01. *Intergovernmental Cooperation.* Nothing in this constitution shall be construed: (1) To prohibit the cooperation of the government of this state with other governments, or (2) the cooperation of the government of any county, city or other civil division with any one or more other governments in the administration of their functions and powers, or (3) the consolidation of existing civil divisions of the state. Any county, city or other civil division may agree, except as limited by general law, to share the costs and responsibilities of functions and services with any one or more other governments.

ARTICLE XII
Constitutional Revision

Section 12.01. *Amending Procedure; Proposals.*

(a) Amendments to this constitution may be proposed by the legislature or by the initiative.

(b) An amendment proposed by the legislature shall be agreed to by record vote of a majority of all of the members, which shall be entered on the journal.

(c) An amendment proposed by the initiative shall be incorporated by its sponsors in an initiative petition which shall contain the full text of the amendment proposed and which shall be signed by qualified voters equal in number to at least _____ per cent of the total votes cast for governor in the last preceding gubernatorial election. Initiative petitions shall be filed with the secretary of the legislature.

(d) An amendment proposed by the initiative shall be presented to the legislature if it is in session and, if it is not in session, when it convenes or reconvenes. If the proposal is agreed to by a majority vote of all the members, such vote shall be entered on the journal and the proposed amendment shall be submitted for adoption in the same manner as amendments proposed by the legislature.

(e) The legislature may provide by law for a procedure for the withdrawal by its sponsors of an initiative petition at any time prior to its submission to the voters.

Section 12.02. *Amendment Procedure; Adoption.*

(a) The question of the adoption of a constitutional amendment shall be submitted to the voters at the first regular or special statewide election held no less than two months after it has been agreed to by the vote of the legislature and, in the case of amendments proposed by the initiative which have failed to receive such legislative approval, not less than two months after the end of the legislative session.

(b) Each proposed constitutional amendment shall be submitted to the voters by a ballot title which shall be descriptive but not argumentative or prejudicial, and which shall be prepared by the legal department of the state, subject to review by the courts. Any amendment submitted to the voters shall become a part of the constitution only when approved by a majority of the votes cast thereon. Each amendment so approved shall take effect thirty days after the date of the vote thereon, unless the amendment itself otherwise provides.

Section 12.03. *Constitutional Conventions.*

(a) The legislature, by an affirmative record vote of a majority of all the members, may at any time submit the question "Shall there be a convention to amend or revise the constitution?" to the qualified voters of the state. If the question of holding a convention is not otherwise submitted to the people at some time during any period of fifteen years, it shall be submitted at the general election in the fifteenth year following the last submission.

(b) The legislature, prior to a popular vote on the holding of a convention, shall provide for a preparatory commission to assemble information on constitutional questions to assist the voters and, if a convention is authorized, the commission shall be continued for the assistance of the delegates. If a majority of the qualified voters voting on the question of holding a convention approves it, delegates shall be chosen at the next regular election not less than three months thereafter unless the legislature shall by law have provided for election of the delegates at the same time that the question is voted on or at a special election.

(c) Any qualified voter of the state shall be eligible to membership in the convention and one delegate shall be elected from each existing legislative district. The convention shall convene not later than one month after the date of the election of delegates and may recess from time to time.

(d) No proposal shall be submitted by the convention to the voters unless it has been printed and upon the desks of the delegates in final form at least three days on which the convention was in session prior to final passage therein, and has received the assent of a majority of all the delegates. The yeas and nays on any question shall, upon request of one-tenth of the delegates present, be entered in the journal. Proposals of the convention shall be submitted to the qualified voters at the first regular or special statewide election not less than two months after final action thereon by the convention, either as a whole or in such parts and with such alternatives as the convention may determine. Any constitutional revision submitted to the voters in accordance with this section shall require the approval of a majority of the qualified voters voting thereon, and shall take effect thirty days after the date of the vote thereon, unless the revision itself otherwise provides.

Section 12.04. *Conflicting Amendments or Revisions.* If conflicting constitutional amendments or revisions submitted to the voters at the same election are approved, the amendment or revision receiving the highest number of affirmative votes shall prevail to the extent of such conflict.

> BICAMERAL ALTERNATIVE: Appropriate changes to reflect passage by two houses must be made throughout this article.

Article XIII
Schedule

Section 13.01. *Effective Date.* This constitution shall be in force from and including the first day of _____, 20__, except as herein otherwise provided.

Section 13.02. *Existing Laws, Rights and Proceedings.* All laws not inconsistent with this constitution shall continue in force until they expire by their own limitation or are amended or repealed, and all existing writs, actions, suits, proceedings, civil or criminal liabilities, prosecutions, judgments, sentences, orders, decrees, appeals, causes of action, contracts, claims, demands, titles and rights shall continue unaffected except as modified in accordance with the provisions of this constitution.

Section 13.03. *Officers.* All officers filling any office by election or appointment shall continue to exercise the duties thereof, according to their respective commissions or appointments, until their offices shall have been abolished or their successors selected and qualified in accordance with this constitution or the laws enacted pursuant thereto.

Section 13.04. *Choice of Officers.* The first election of governor under this constitution shall be in 20__. The first election of members of the legislature under this constitution shall be in 20__.

Section 13.05. *Establishment of the Legislature.* Until otherwise provided by law, members of the legislature shall be elected from the following districts: The first district shall consist of [the description of all the districts from which the first legislature will be elected should be inserted here].

BICAMERAL ALTERNATIVE: Section 13.05. *Establishment of the Legislature.* Refer to "assembly districts" and "senate districts."

Section 13.06. *Administrative Reorganization.* The governor shall submit to the legislature orders embodying a plan for reorganization of administrative departments in accordance with Section 5.06 of this constitution prior to [date]. These orders shall become effective as originally issued or as they may be modified by law on [a date three months later] unless any of them are made effective at earlier dates by law.

Section 13.07. *Establishment of the Judiciary.*

(a) The unified judicial system shall be inaugurated on September 15, 20__. Prior to that date the judges and principal ministerial agents of the judicial system shall be designated or selected and any other act needed to prepare for the operation of the system shall be done in accordance with this constitution.

(b) The judicial power vested in any court in the state shall be transferred to the unified judicial system and the justices and judges of the [here name all the courts of the state except justice of the peace courts] holding office on September 15, 20__, shall become judges of the unified judicial system and shall continue to serve as such for the remainder of their respective terms and until their successors shall have qualified. The justices of the [here name the highest court of the state] shall become judges of the supreme court and the judges of the other courts shall be assigned by the chief judge to appropriate service in the other departments of the judicial system, due regard being had to their positions in the existing judicial structure and to the districts in which they had been serving.

– – – –

Editor's Note: Additional information on state constitutions may be obtained from The Council of State Governments, P.O.Box 11910, Lexington, Kentucky 40578-1910, telephone (859) 244-8105, or directly from their website (http://www.csg.org/).

Federal Government

Edwin Meese III

The Constitution defines, directly or indirectly, the structure and responsibilities of the federal government. According to the Constitution, any power not specifically given to the federal government is a power of the states. The country has changed tremendously since 1787 when the Founding Fathers wrote the Constitution. Changing circumstances have made it necessary to amend or change the Constitution and to expand the federal government. The principles behind the government have not changed even though the federal government has grown.

The Executive Branch

Of the three branches of the government, the **executive** branch is perhaps the most complex. Its job is to enforce the laws of the United States. It is made up of:

- the President;
- the Vice President;

Originally published as "The Federal Government," U.S. Government Structure, 1987. Published by the Emigration and Naturalization Service, U.S. Department of Justice, U.S. Government Printing Office, Washington, D.C.

- the executive departments; and,
- the independent agencies.

Each has special powers and functions. These are the general powers:

- The President acts as leader of the country and Commander in Chief of the military. He or she directs the federal government and enforces federal laws.
- The Vice President **presides** over the Senate and votes in case of a tie. He or she becomes President if the President is disabled or otherwise cannot serve.
- The departments, and their heads, the **Cabinet** members, advise the President on specific policy issues and help carry out those policies.
- The independent agencies help carry out policy or provide special services.

THE PRESIDENT

The Presidency is the highest office in the country. According to the Constitution, the President must:

- be a natural-born citizen of the United States;
- be at least 35 years old by the time he/she will serve; and,
- have lived in the United States at least 14 years.

If a person meets these qualifications, he or she may run for President in the election.

Presidential elections occur every four years. Presidential **candidates** are chosen by their **political parties** in the months before the election. A political party is a group of people who have similar ideas about how the government should be run. Each party chooses its candidates in the following way:

- Each party holds **primary elections**, conventions or caucuses in every state.
— The candidates **campaign** and
— The people who belong to each party vote for the person they believe would be the best candidate; and,

- Each party holds a national convention.
  — Party members meet to choose the candidates for President and Vice President.
  — The Presidential candidate is usually the person who has won the most primary elections or conventions.
  — All states are included in the national convention of the party.

Some parties are too small to have primaries. They hold conventions to choose their candidates. The **Republican** and **Democratic** parties are the largest in the United States, but there are many smaller political parties. Candidates for public office also may be independent; that is, they do not have to belong to a political party.

After all candidates are chosen, the campaign begins for the **general election**. The winner of that election becomes President. The procedure for the general election is as follows:

- It is always held on the first Tuesday *after* the first Monday in November;
- People in each state vote *indirectly* for their choice for President:
  — the **Electoral College** actually elects the President;
  — the people vote to choose electors who will vote for the President candidate;
  — the number of electors is the same as the number of Representatives plus the number of Senators the state has;
  — in this way, the states keep their **influence** over the election of the President;
- The electors from each state meet on a specified date:
  — they do not vote for the person they want to be President;
  — they vote for the choice of the largest number of people in their state; and,
- The candidate with more than half of the electoral votes wins. (If no candidate has more than half of the electoral votes, the House of Representatives chooses one of the candidates.)

The newly elected President is **inaugurated** on January 20, two months after the November election. Each President may serve only two terms. Each term is four years.

The President has many duties and responsibilities, most of which are listed in the Constitution. The main ones are:

- to enforce laws and treaties of the United States;
- to conduct **foreign policy** (subject to certain limits placed by Congress and the Constitution);
- to serve as Commander in Chief of the armed forces;
- to approve or **veto** the bills which Congress passes;
- when appropriate, to **pardon** people found guilty of breaking federal law;
- to appoint people to certain positions, subject to Senate approval:
  — heads of executive departments, or Cabinet members;
  — heads of independent executive agencies;
  — Supreme Court justices and judges of other federal courts; and,
- to advise Congress on his/her perception of the nation's needs.

THE VICE PRESIDENT

The Vice-Presidency is the second highest office in the country, next to the President. If the President dies, leaves office, or cannot perform his/her duties, the Vice President becomes President. For this reason, the Vice President must meet the same requirements as the President:

- be a natural-born citizen of the U.S.;
- be at least 35 years old by the time he or she will serve; and,
- have lived in the United States at least 14 years.

The Constitution established that the Vice President would be the person who received the second highest number of electoral votes, but that did not work well. Often the person who received the second highest number of votes had been the **opponent** of the person who had the most votes. When they became President and Vice President, they could not always work well together. The 12th amendment, in 1804, established separate ballots in the Electoral College for President and Vice President. First the electors vote on the President and then the Vice President. The President and Vice President run together in the general election.

The Vice President has special duties and responsibilities, most of which are listed in the Constitution. The most important ones are:

- to serve as Acting President if the President is disabled, for example, during an operation;

• to preside over the Senate, and vote in case of a tie;
• to act as a link between the President and the Senate;
• to participate in **Cabinet** meetings; and,
• to serve as a member of the National Security Council.

Laws also have been passed to establish a **succession** to the Presidency, in the event that both the President and the Vice President are unable to serve. The next in line, after the Vice President, is the Speaker of the House of Representatives, then the President **pro tempore** of the Senate, then the Secretary of State. The **line of succession** then includes the other Cabinet members in a set order. This order makes certain that the country will never be without a leader. The descriptions of the executive departments which follow are in the same order as the line of succession.

THE CABINET

The members of the Cabinet are the heads of the executive departments and usually are called **Secretaries**. (The head of the Department of Justice is the **Attorney General of the U.S.**) The Constitution did not set up a cabinet, but every President, beginning with George Washington, has had a Cabinet to advise him and to carry out his instructions. The Cabinet and the departments are very helpful in carrying out the policies of the government which affect almost everyone living in the United States.

During George Washington's Presidency, there were only four Cabinet members: Secretary of State, Secretary of Treasury, Secretary of War, and Attorney General. As of 1987 there were 13 departments, showing how much the nation has grown and changed. Perhaps in the future more departments will be added or some will be **abolished**. This will depend on the needs of the nation. The 13 departments and their main responsibilities are:

DEPARTMENT OF STATE

• Advises the President in making and conducting foreign policy.
• Provides information and advice about other countries.
• Provides services to Americans traveling or living abroad.

- Conducts consular affairs and services, such as providing visas.
- **Negotiates** treaties and agreements with other countries.

DEPARTMENT OF THE TREASURY

- Advises the President on financial matters.
- Operates the Customs Service which regulates exports from and imports to the U.S.
- Designs and prints currency and makes coins.
- Maintains the Secret Service which provides protection to high-ranking government officials.
- Finds and arrests banking and currency law violators.
- Operates the Internal Revenue Service which collects income taxes.

DEPARTMENT OF DEFENSE

- Advises the President on military matters.
- Provides military forces to protect national security.
- Responsible for national defense.
- Directs the Army, Air Force and Navy, including the Marine Corps.

DEPARTMENT OF JUSTICE

- Advises the President on legal matters.
- Protects rights guaranteed by the Constitution.
- Represents the United States in all legal matters.
- Conducts cases in the Supreme Court if the U.S. is involved.
- Through the Immigration and Naturalization Service, enforces immigration laws and provides information and processes applications for immigrants who wish to become citizens.
- Maintains the federal prison system.

Department of the Interior

- Advises the President on conservation issues.
- Maintains most nationally owned public lands and natural resources.
- Administers programs for Native American groups.
- Works to identify, protect and restore endangered species of fish, wildlife and plants.
- Administers the national parks, monuments, historic sites and recreation areas through the National Park Service.

Department of Agriculture

- Advises the President on problems of farmers.
- Researches efficient agricultural methods.
- Provides loans to help family-size and smaller farms.
- Inspects and grades agricultural produce, such as meat and poultry, which appears in the grocery store.
- Provides nutrition programs for low-income persons.
- Helps farmers get a fair price for their crops.
- Operates national forests.

Department of Commerce

- Advises the President about the country's business matters.
- Promotes and develops domestic and foreign trade.
- Conducts the **Census** every 10 years.
- Issues patents.
- Studies transportation and travel.
- Provides weather reports to the public.

Department of Labor

- Advises the President on the welfare of workers.

- Administers labor laws to ensure safe and healthful working conditions, minimum wage laws, overtime pay rates, freedom from employment **discrimination**, unemployment insurance, and workers' compensation.
- Administers job training programs to help disadvantaged persons attain self-sufficiency.
- Protects rights of union members.

DEPARTMENT OF HEALTH AND HUMAN SERVICES

- Advises the President on health and welfare policies and programs.
- Works to improve health services.
- Works to prevent and control disease.
- Administers assistance programs, such as Social Security, Aid to Families with Dependent Children, Aid to the Blind, and refugee assistance programs.

DEPARTMENT OF HOUSING AND URBAN DEVELOPMENT

- Advises the President on housing programs and community development.
- Works to improve housing and living conditions.
- Provides low interest loans to promote home ownership and development of low cost housing.

DEPARTMENT OF TRANSPORTATION

- Advises the President on transportation matters.
- Develops policies and programs to promote safe, fast, convenient and efficient transportation.
- Maintains the Coast Guard which enforces safety **regulations** for vessels, and saves lives and property at sea.
- Promotes development of air transportation, highways, and railroads.

DEPARTMENT OF EDUCATION

- Advises the President on education programs and plans.
- Works to improve education in the U.S.
- Provides support for special education.
- Publishes reports on the condition of education.
- Administers programs providing educational services, such as bilingual, vocational and adult education.
- Assists many students in paying for post-secondary schooling through grants, loans and work study programs.

DEPARTMENT OF ENERGY

- Advises the President on energy planning and policy making.
- Researches new, efficient and cost-effective forms of energy.
- Promotes conservation of energy.
- Researches and provides information on energy trends.
- Regulates energy rates and grants licenses.

DEPARTMENT OF VETERANS AFFAIRS[1]

- Advises the President on matters relating to veterans affairs.
- Provides services to veterans of all branches of the armed services.
- Services include burial and memorial benefits, health benefits and services, compensation and pension benefits, vocational rehabilitation and employment services, home loan and guaranty services, life insurance programs, and educational benefits.
- Administers all special veterans programs, such as those for disabled veterans, homeless veterans, military veterans, minority veterans, and women veterans.
- Supervises all federal agencies that provide government services to veterans.
- Protects the rights of veterans under all laws pertaining to their services and benefits.

- Manages and processes appeals of veterans under the Board of Veterans Appeals.

It should be noted that Congress, in December of 2002, created the newest federal department, the Department of Homeland Security. For information about this department please refer to the White House home page <http://www.whitehouse.gov/homeland/>.

INDEPENDENT AGENCIES

In addition to the departments, there are independent agencies in the executive branch. They are not departments because they serve a very specific need or they are intended to be temporary. There are dozens of agencies, and they change more frequently than departments. Some of these agencies and their main responsibilities are:

- **Commission on Civil Rights** tries to prevent discrimination on the basis of race, color, religion, sex, age, handicapping condition, or national origin.
- **Consumer Product Safety Commission** investigates and reports on the safety of consumer products.
- **Environmental Protection Agency** sets standards for clean air and water; helps industry and local government clean up polluted areas.
- **Federal Deposit Insurance Company** (FDIC) insures the money deposited in banks which belong to the FDIC system.
- **Federal Election Commission** (FEC) tries to keep elections to federal office honest and fair.
- **Federal Reserve Board** helps the nation's economy grow, by controlling the money. The Federal Reserve loans money only to banks.
- **Federal Trade Commission** (FTC) promotes fair competition in the economy.
- **National Aeronautics and Space Administration** (NASA) promotes and develops programs which are devoted to the peaceful use of space. NASA plans and carries out all space flights, including the space shuttle, and works to develop the space station program.
- **National Labor Relations Board** attempts to protect the rights of both employer and employee to have fair labor relations.

- **Small Business Administration** (SBA) counsels, assists and protects small business interests. The SBA provides loans, education and assistance to small businesses.
- **United States Information Agency** (USIA) publicizes aspects of U.S. culture, policy and opinions abroad to encourage understanding of the U.S. in other countries. It produces Voice of America and Radio Marti broadcasts.
- **United States Postal Service** is responsible for delivering nearly 150 billion pieces of mail throughout the U.S. each year.
- **Veterans Administration** (VA) provides services to men and women who served in the U.S. armed forces. The VA helps veterans and their families with education, loans, medical services, and **compensation** to disabled veterans or to the families of those who died.

The Legislative Branch

The legislative branch, or Congress, makes the laws which govern the nation. Congress is divided into two houses, the **Senate** and the **House of Representatives**. This is called a **bicameral** legislature. The House and Senate have some separate and some shared responsibilities. The shared duties and responsibilities as written in the Constitution are:

- regulating money and trade, including
  - printing or coining of money,
  - borrowing of money by the government,
  - **levying** and collecting taxes, and,
  - regulating trade between states and with foreign countries;
- providing for the national defense, including
  - maintaining the Army, Navy and Air Force, and
  - declaring war;
- making laws regarding naturalization of persons seeking citizenship;
- establishing post offices;
- regulating the system of weights and measures; and,
- passing laws to govern the District of Columbia, the nation's capital.

The separate responsibilities, as written in the Constitution, are:

- **House of Representatives:**
  — introducing bills about the budget or taxes,
  — **impeaching** officials; and,
- **Senate:**
  — determining if impeached officials are innocent or guilty,
  — confirming Presidential **appointments**, and
  — ratifying treaties between the U.S. and other governments.

The Constitution also lists some things Congress may **never** do:

- tax exports;
- pass trade laws which do not treat all states equally;
- spend tax money without a law to authorize it;
- authorize any title of nobility;
- pass a law to punish someone for an act which was legal when the person did it; and,
- pass any law which takes away a person's right to a trial in court.

Passing a Law

Congress spends most of its time passing **legislation** or laws. A complex procedure is followed to make sure that many different people have a chance to discuss the **bill**, ask questions about it, and change (amend) it if they think it needs to be changed. The procedure is as follows:

- Either a Senator or a Representative may introduce a bill which he/she wants to become a law.
  — The *exception* is that only Representatives may introduce tax or budget bills.
- A **committee** of the **House of Congress** in which the bill was introduced studies the bill. The bill can be:
  — amended,
  — rewritten,
  — recommended for passage without changes,
  — **tabled** or ignored, or
  — reported back to its House with no recommendation, after which it usually does not become law.

- Unless tabled the bill goes to its House of Congress for **debate**.
  — The committee makes a report on the bill.
  — The House debates and amends the bill, if needed.
  — The House either passes or defeats the bill.
- If the bill passes the first House, it is sent to the other House.
  — The second House debates the bill.
  — If the bill is amended, it must be sent back to the first House. Both Houses of Congress must agree on the amendments.
- If the bill passes both Houses in the same form, it is sent to the President. He can:
  — sign it. Then it becomes law.
  — do nothing. After 10 days, if Congress stays in session, it becomes law.
  — do nothing. If Congress **adjourns** within 10 days, it does not become law.
  — veto it. It does not become law.
- Congress may pass the bill over the President's veto by a two-thirds vote of both Houses.

STRUCTURE

The two Houses of Congress are set up very differently. (See the United States History book, chapter IV.) The Senate is the smaller House. Its structure and requirements for serving are explained below.

- The Senate has 100 members (Senators).
  — There are two from every state.
  — Each Senator represents the whole state.
  — Members are elected for six-year terms.
  — Elections for one-third of the Senate seats are held every two years.
  — There is no limit to the number of times a Senator may be re-elected.
- Its officers include:
  — the Vice President, who presides and votes only in case of a tie, and
  — the President pro tempore, a Senator chosen to preside when the Vice President is not there.
- To be a Senator, a person must be:
  — at least 30 years old,
  — a citizen at least nine years, and,
  — a resident of the state he/she represents.

The House of Representatives is set up differently from the Senate. It also has different qualifications.

- The House of Representatives has 435 members (Representatives).
  - The number of Representatives from each state varies, and this number is based on the population.
    - Each state has at least one Representative.
    - The District of Columbia has one Representatives who does not vote.
  - Most states are divided into districts. A Representative of the people is chosen in each district.
  - Members are elected for two-year terms.
  - There is no limit to the number of times a Representative may be re-elected.
- The Speaker of the House presides.
  - The Speaker of the House is elected by the other Representatives.
  - The Speaker is usually a member of the majority party.
- To be a Representative, a person must be:
  - at least 25 years old,
  - a citizen at least seven years, and
  - a resident of the state he/she represents.

The Constitution established that the Congress must meet regularly. A new Congress begins every two years, with the election of new Senators and Representatives. The time they meet to make laws is called a **session**. Congress meets in the Capitol Building in Washington, D.C. The House of Representatives has a large room, the Senate a smaller one, and the President has some offices for his/her use. Many people visit the Capitol Building each year to see where their members of Congress make laws.

The Judicial Branch

The judicial branch is made up of different federal courts. It is responsible for explaining and interpreting the laws. People take cases to court to preserve the rights guaranteed to them in the Constitution and by law. They also can take cases to court if they believe the laws passed by Congress or by a state are **unconstitutional**.

STRUCTURE

The court structure in the United States is **hierarchical**. There are local, state and federal courts, as well as different courts for different purposes. The establishment of the federal courts is provided in Article III of the Constitution, but most of the structure was decided later.

- The **Supreme Court** is the highest court in the country.
  — It was established by the Constitution.
  — Its **ruling** is the final decision on a case.
- **Circuit Courts of Appeals** are the second highest courts, a step below the Supreme Court.
  — There are 11 Circuit Courts in the United States.
  — They hear **appeals** from lower courts, when people believe something was unjust about the decision of the lower court.
- **District Courts** are the lowest level of federal courts.
  — As of 1987, there were 94 district courts in the United States.
  — If a person is accused of breaking a federal law, he/she will be tried in a district court.
- Congress also has set up some **special courts**:
  — Court of Claims,
  — Customs Court,
  — Court of Customs and Patent Appeals, and
  — Court of Military Appeals.

The federal courts have special duties:

- to explain the meaning of the Constitution, laws of the United States and treaties;
- to settle legal disputes between citizens of different states;
- to settle legal disagreements between two or more states;
- to settle legal questions between states and the federal government;
- to settle legal disagreements between individuals and the federal government;
- to settle disagreements between states and foreign governments or their citizens; and,
- to naturalize persons as United States citizens.

THE SUPREME COURT

The Supreme Court — the highest court in the United States — cannot be abolished except by amending the Constitution. Nine judges, called **Justices**, sit on the Supreme Court in Washington, D.C. One of the judges is chosen as **Chief Justice**, who acts as the leader. The Supreme Court has two types of authority:

- As an **appellate court**, it can overturn decision made by lower courts.
  — Most cases it hears are appeals, in which people believe the decision of a lower court was not fair.
  — The *exception* is that cases involving foreign diplomats originate in the Supreme Court.
- As the Supreme Court, it can declare a state or federal law unconstitutional.
  — That means the law disagrees with the Constitution and must be abolished.
  — The decision is final.

APPEALS

One of the most important rights in the United States is the right to a fair trial. The appeals process is set up to help make sure that people have as fair a trial as possible. Sometimes a person believes justice was not served at his/her trial because he/she believes:

- his/her rights were violated;
- a rule of law was not properly followed; or,
- all the evidence was not available.

That person may try to appeal his/her case to a higher court. The judge may agree with the:

- person and overturn the lower court's decision; or,
- lower court and uphold the decision.

The person may try to appeal again if he/she still is not satisfied. Courts will not always hear appeals, however. The Supreme Court does not hear all appeals because:

- the Supreme Court is busy, and wants to be able to give enough time to each case;
- it usually hears cases which involve complex questions about the protection of rights; and,
- sometimes the Justices decide in a **preliminary** review that the lower court gave the right decision.

Make It Work

The United States government seems complicated to many people because it has so many parts. Each branch has its specific functions. The branches work together to make a government which can best serve the interests of all the people. The three branches make the system of government by law work:

- the **legislative branch** makes the laws;
- the **executive branch** puts the laws into effect; and,
- the **judicial branch** applies and explains the laws.

Just as the three branches work together, they also serve to **check and balance** each other. This important principle was written into the Constitution so that the branches would have the same amount of power. There are several ways the branches check and balance each other:

- The Supreme Court can declare a law passed by the Congress or an action by the President to be unconstitutional.
- The President can veto a law passed by Congress.
- Congress can pass a law **overriding** the President's veto.
- The President appoints Supreme Court Justices.
- Congress can refuse to confirm appointments made by the President.

Responsibilities

Both citizens and the government have responsibilities to each other. It is important for each to fulfill their responsibilities. Some citizen responsibilities are to:

- be an informed and regular voter;
- obey laws;
- pay taxes honestly and on time; and,
- express concern and requests about the government in a peaceful and helpful way.

Some government responsibilities are to:

- protect and enforce the rights guaranteed in the Constitution;
- spend people's tax money wisely; and,
- be responsive to citizens' requests.

The constitution defines, directly or indirectly, both the structure and responsibilities of the U.S. federal government. This includes all departments, agencies, quasi-independent, and independent organizations. While the public is aware of the three main branches of their national government — legislative, executive, and judicial — the wording of the U.S. Constitution, explicitly or implicitly, permits these other aspects of the American national government to exist. These powers are enumerated in the U.S. Constitution itself, the Bill of Rights, and subsequent amendments to the federal constitution. (Last paragraph added by Editor.)

– – – –

Editor's Note: A copy of this entire book, *U.S. Government Structure* (1987), may be obtained from the U.S. Government Printing Office, P.O. Box 371954, Pittsburgh, Pennsylvania 15250-7954, or may be ordered over the internet from GPO's online bookstore (http://bookstore.gpo.gov). Another excellent book, *Our American Government* (1993), is also available from this same source.

MODEL FEDERAL GOVERNMENT CHARTER[2]
The Constitution of the United States

We the people of the United States, in order to form a more perfect union, establish justice, insure domestic tranquility, provide for the common defense, promote the general welfare, and secure the blessings of liberty to ourselves and our posterity, do ordain and establish this Constitution for the United States of America.

ARTICLE I

Section 1. All legislative powers herein granted shall be vested in a Congress of the United States, which shall consist of a Senate and House of Representatives.

Section 2. The House of Representatives shall be composed of members chosen every second year by the people of the several states, and the electors in each state shall have the qualifications requisite for electors of the most numerous branch of the state legislature.

No person shall be a Representative who shall not have attained to the age of twenty five years, and been seven years a citizen of the United States, and who shall not, when elected, be an inhabitant of that state in which he shall be chosen.

Representatives and direct taxes shall be apportioned among the several states which may be included within this union, according to their respective numbers, which shall be determined by adding to the whole number of free persons, including those bound to service for a term of years, and excluding Indians not taxed, three fifths of all other Persons. The actual Enumeration shall be made within three years after the first meeting of the Congress of the United States, and within every subsequent term of ten years, in such manner as they shall by law direct. The number of Representatives shall not exceed one for every thirty thousand, but each state shall have at least one Representative; and until such enumeration shall be made, the state of New Hampshire shall be entitled to chuse three, Massachusetts eight, Rhode Island and Providence Plantations one,

Connecticut five, New York six, New Jersey four, Pennsylvania eight, Delaware one, Maryland six, Virginia ten, North Carolina five, South Carolina five, and Georgia three.

When vacancies happen in the Representation from any state, the executive authority thereof shall issue writs of election to fill such vacancies.

The House of Representatives shall choose their speaker and other officers; and shall have the sole power of impeachment.

Section 3. The Senate of the United States shall be composed of two Senators from each state, chosen by the legislature thereof, for six years; and each Senator shall have one vote.

Immediately after they shall be assembled in consequence of the first election, they shall be divided as equally as may be into three classes. The seats of the Senators of the first class shall be vacated at the expiration of the second year, of the second class at the expiration of the fourth year, and the third class at the expiration of the sixth year, so that one third may be chosen every second year; and if vacancies happen by resignation, or otherwise, during the recess of the legislature of any state, the executive thereof may make temporary appointments until the next meeting of the legislature, which shall then fill such vacancies.

No person shall be a Senator who shall not have attained to the age of thirty years, and been nine years a citizen of the United States and who shall not, when elected, be an inhabitant of that state for which he shall be chosen.

The Vice President of the United States shall be President of the Senate, but shall have no vote, unless they be equally divided.

The Senate shall choose their other officers, and also a President pro tempore, in the absence of the Vice President, or when he shall exercise the office of President of the United States.

The Senate shall have the sole power to try all impeachments. When sitting for that purpose, they shall be on oath or affirmation. When the President of the United States is tried, the Chief Justice shall preside: And no person shall be convicted without the concurrence of two thirds of the members present.

Judgment in cases of impeachment shall not extend further than to removal from office, and disqualification to hold and enjoy any office of honor, trust or profit under the United States: but the party convicted shall nevertheless be liable and subject to indictment, trial, judgment and punishment, according to law.

Section 4. The times, places and manner of holding elections for Senators and Representatives, shall be prescribed in each state by the legislature thereof; but the Congress may at any time by law make or alter such regulations, except as to the places of choosing Senators.

The Congress shall assemble at least once in every year, and such meeting shall be on the first Monday in December, unless they shall by law appoint a different day.

Section 5. Each House shall be the judge of the elections, returns and qualifications of its own members, and a majority of each shall constitute a quorum to do business; but a smaller number may adjourn from day to day, and may be authorized to compel the attendance of absent members, in such manner, and under such penalties as each House may provide.

Each House may determine the rules of its proceedings, punish its members for disorderly behavior, and, with the concurrence of two thirds, expel a member.

Each House shall keep a journal of its proceedings, and from time to time publish the same, excepting such parts as may in their judgment require secrecy; and the yeas and nays of the members of either House on any question shall, at the desire of one fifth of those present, be entered on the journal.

Neither House, during the session of Congress, shall, without the consent of the other, adjourn for more than three days, nor to any other place than that in which the two Houses shall be sitting.

Section 6. The Senators and Representatives shall receive a compensation for their services, to be ascertained by law, and paid out of the treasury of the United States. They shall in all cases, except treason, felony and breach of the peace, be privileged from arrest during their attendance at the session of their respective Houses, and in going to and returning from the same; and for any speech or debate in either House, they shall not be questioned in any other place.

No Senator or Representative shall, during the time for which he was elected, be appointed to any civil office under the authority of the United States, which shall have been created, or the emoluments whereof shall have been increased during such time: and no person holding any office under the United States, shall be a member of either House during his continuance in office.

Section 7. All bills for raising revenue shall originate in the House of Representatives; but the Senate may propose or concur with amendments as on other Bills.

Every bill which shall have passed the House of Representatives and the Senate, shall, before it become a law, be presented to the President of the United States; if he approve he shall sign it, but if not he shall return it, with his objections to that House in which it shall have originated, who shall enter the objections at large on their journal, and proceed to reconsider it. If after such reconsideration two thirds of that House shall agree to pass the bill, it shall be sent, together with the objections, to the other by which it shall likewise be reconsidered, and if approved by two thirds of that House, it shall become a law. But in all such cases the votes of both Houses shall be determined by yeas and nays, and the names of the persons voting for and against the bill shall be entered on the journal of each House respectively. If any bill shall not be returned by the President within ten days (Sundays excepted) after it shall have been presented to him, the same shall be a law, in like manner as if he had signed it, unless the Congress by their adjournment prevent its return, in which case it shall not be a law.

Every order, resolution, or vote to which the concurrence of the Senate and House of Representatives may be necessary (except on a question of adjournment) shall be presented to the President of the United States; and before the same shall take effect, shall be approved by him, or being disapproved by him, shall be repassed by two thirds of the Senate and House of Representatives, according to the rules and limitations prescribed in the case of a bill.

Section 8. The Congress shall have power to lay and collect taxes, duties, imposts and excises, to pay debts and provide for the common defense and general welfare of the United States; but all duties, imposts and excises shall be uniform throughout the United States;

To borrow money on the credit of the United States;

To regulate commerce with foreign nations, and among the several states, and with the Indian tribes;

To establish a uniform rule of naturalization, and uniform laws on the subject of bankruptcies throughout the United States;

To coin money, regulate the value thereof, and of foreign coin, and fix the standard of weights and measures;

To provide for the punishment of counterfeiting the securities and current coin of the United States;

To establish post offices and post roads;

To promote the progress of science and useful arts, by securing for limited times to authors and inventors the exclusive right to their respective writings and discoveries;

To constitute tribunals inferior to the Supreme Court;

To define and punish piracies and felonies committed on the high seas, and offenses against the law of nations;

To declare war, grant letters of marque and reprisal, and make rules concerning captures on land and water;

To raise and support armies, but no appropriation of money to that use shall be for a longer term than two years;

To provide and maintain a navy;

To make rules for the government and regulation of the land and naval forces;

To provide for calling forth the militia to execute the laws of the union, suppress insurrections and repel invasions;

To provide for organizing, arming, and disciplining, the militia, and for governing such part of them as may be employed in the service of the United States, reserving to the states respectively, the appointment of the officers, and the authority of training the militia according to the discipline prescribed by Congress;

To exercise exclusive legislation in all cases whatsoever, over such District (not exceeding ten miles square) as may, by cession of particular states, and the acceptance of Congress, become the seat of the government of the United States, and to exercise like authority over all places purchased by the consent of the legislature of the state in which the same shall be, for the erection of forts, magazines, arsenals, dockyards, and other needful buildings; — And

To make all laws which shall be necessary and proper for carrying into execution the foregoing powers, and all other powers vested by this Constitution in the government of the United States, or in any department or officer thereof.

Section 9. The migration or importation of such persons as any of the states now existing shall think proper to admit, shall not be prohibited by the Congress prior to the year one thousand eight hundred and eight, but a tax or duty may be imposed on such importation, not exceeding ten dollars for each person.

The privilege of the writ of habeas corpus shall not be suspended, unless when in cases of rebellion or invasion the public safety may require it.

No bill of attainder or ex post facto Law shall be passed.

No capitation, or other direct, tax shall be laid, unless in proportion to the census or enumeration herein before directed to be taken.

No tax or duty shall be laid on articles exported from any state.

No preference shall be given by any regulation of commerce or revenue to the ports of one state over those of another: nor shall vessels bound to, or from, one state, be obliged to enter, clear or pay duties in another.

No money shall be drawn from the treasury, but in consequence of appropriations made by law; and a regular statement and account of receipts and expenditures of all public money shall be published from time to time.

No title of nobility shall be granted by the United States: and no person holding any office of profit or trust under them, shall, without the consent of the Congress, accept of any present, emolument, office, or title, of any kind whatever, from any king, prince, or foreign state.

Section 10. No state shall enter into any treaty, alliance, or confederation; grant letters of marque and reprisal; coin money; emit bills of credit; make anything but gold and silver coin a tender in payment of debts; pass any bill of attainder, ex post facto law, or law impairing the obligation of contracts, or grant any title of nobility.

No state shall, without the consent of the Congress, lay any imposts or duties on imports or exports, except what may be absolutely necessary for executing its inspection laws: and the net produce of all duties and imposts, laid by any state on imports or exports, shall be for the use of the treasury of the United States; and all such laws shall be subject to the revision and control of the Congress.

No state shall, without the consent of Congress, lay any duty of tonnage, keep troops, or ships of war in time of peace, enter into any agreement or compact with another state, or with a foreign power, or engage in war, unless actually invaded, or in such imminent danger as will not admit of delay.

ARTICLE II

Section 1. The executive power shall be vested in a President of the United States of America. He shall hold his office during the term of four years, and, together with the Vice President, chosen for the same term, be elected, as follows:

Each state shall appoint, in such manner as the Legislature thereof may direct, a number of electors, equal to the whole number of Senators and Representatives to which the State may be entitled in the Congress:

but no Senator or Representative, or person holding an office of trust or profit under the United States, shall be appointed an elector.

The electors shall meet in their respective states, and vote by ballot for two persons, of whom one at least shall not be an inhabitant of the same state with themselves. And they shall make a list of all the persons voted for, and of the number of votes for each; which list they shall sign and certify, and transmit sealed to the seat of the government of the United States, directed to the President of the Senate. The President of the Senate shall, in the presence of the Senate and House of Representatives, open all the certificates, and the votes shall then be counted. The person having the greatest number of votes shall be the President, if such number be a majority of the whole number of electors appointed; and if there be more than one who have such majority, and have an equal number of votes, then the House of Representatives shall immediately choose by ballot one of them for President; and if no person have a majority, then from the five highest on the list the said House shall in like manner choose the President. But in choosing the President, the votes shall be taken by States, the representation from each state have one vote; A quorum for this purpose shall consist of a member or members from two thirds of the states, and a majority of all the states shall be necessary to a choice. In every case, after the choice of the President, the person having the greatest number of votes of the electors shall be the Vice President. But if there should remain two or more who have equal votes, the Senate shall choose from them by ballot the Vice President.

The Congress may determine the time of choosing the electors, and the day on which they shall give their votes; which day shall be the same throughout the United States.

No person except a natural born citizen, or a citizen of the United States, at the time of the adoption of this Constitution, shall be eligible to the office of President; neither shall any person be eligible to that office who shall not have attained to the age of thirty five years, and been fourteen Years a resident within the United States.

In case of the removal of the President from office, or of his death, resignation, or inability to discharge the powers and duties of the said office, the same shall devolve on the Vice President, and the Congress may by law provide for the case of removal, death, resignation or inability, both of the President and Vice President, declaring what officer shall then act as President, and such officer shall act accordingly, until the disability be removed, or a President shall be elected.

The President shall, at stated times, receive for his services, a compensation, which shall neither be increased nor diminished during the period for which he shall have been elected, and he shall not receive within that period any other emolument from the United States, or any of them.

Before he enter on the execution of his office, he shall take the following oath or affirmation: — "I do solemnly swear (or affirm) that I will faithfully execute the office of President of the United States, and will to the best of my ability, preserve, protect and defend the Constitution of the United States."

Section 2. The President shall be commander in chief of the Army and Navy of the United States, and of the militia of the several states, when called into the actual service of the United States; he may require the opinion, in writing, of the principal officer in each of the executive departments, upon any subject relating to the duties of their respective offices, and he shall have power to grant reprieves and pardons for offenses against the United States, except in cases of impeachment.

He shall have power, by and with the advice and consent of the Senate, to make treaties, provided two thirds of the Senators present concur; and he shall nominate, and by and with the advice and consent of the Senate, shall appoint ambassadors, other public ministers and consuls, judges of the Supreme Court, and all other officers of the United States, whose appointments are not herein otherwise provided for, and which shall be established by law: but the Congress may by law vest the appointment of such inferior officers, as they think proper, in the President alone, in the courts of law, or in the heads of departments.

The President shall have power to fill up all vacancies that may happen during the recess of the Senate, by granting commissions which shall expire at the end of their next session.

Section 3. He shall from time to time give to the Congress information of the state of the union, and recommend to their consideration such measures as he shall judge necessary and expedient; he may, on extraordinary occasions, convene both Houses, or either of them, and in case of disagreement between them, with respect to the time of adjournment, he may adjourn them to such time as he shall think proper; he shall receive ambassadors and other public ministers; he shall take care that the laws be faithfully executed, and shall commission all the officers of the United States.

Section 4. The President, Vice President and all civil officers of the United States, shall be removed from office on impeachment for, and conviction of, treason, bribery, or other high crimes and misdemeanors.

ARTICLE III

Section 1. The judicial power of the United States, shall be vested in one Supreme Court, and in such inferior courts as the Congress may from time to time ordain and establish. The judges, both of the supreme and inferior courts, shall hold their offices during good behaviour, and shall, at stated times, receive for their services, a compensation, which shall not be diminished during their continuance in office.

Section 2. The judicial power shall extend to all cases, in law and equity, arising under this Constitution, the laws of the United States, and treaties made, or which shall be made, under their authority; — to all cases affecting ambassadors, other public ministers and consuls; — to all cases of admiralty and maritime jurisdiction; — to controversies to which the United States shall be a party; — to controversies between two or more states; — between a state and citizens of another state; — between citizens of different states; — between citizens of the same state claiming lands under grants of different states, and between a state, or the citizens thereof, and foreign states, citizens or subjects.

In all cases affecting ambassadors, other public ministers and consuls, and those in which a state shall be party, the Supreme Court shall have original jurisdiction. In all the other cases before mentioned, the Supreme Court shall have appellate jurisdiction, both as to law and fact, with such exceptions, and under such regulations as the Congress shall make.

The trial of all crimes, except in cases of impeachment, shall be by jury; and such trial shall be held in the state where the said crimes shall have been committed; but when not committed within any state, the trial shall be at such place or places as the Congress may by law have directed.

Section 3. Treason against the United States, shall consist only in levying war against them, or in adhering to their enemies, giving them aid and comfort. No person shall be convicted of treason unless on the testimony of two witnesses to the same overt act, or on confession in open court.

The Congress shall have power to declare the punishment of treason, but no attainder of treason shall work corruption of blood, or forfeiture except during the life of the person attainted.

ARTICLE IV

Section 1. Full faith and credit shall be given in each state to the public acts, records, and judicial proceedings of every other state. And the

Congress may by general laws prescribe the manner in which such acts, records, and proceedings shall be proved, and the effect thereof.

Section 2. The citizens of each state shall be entitled to all privileges and immunities of citizens in the several states.

A person charged in any state with treason, felony, or other crime, who shall flee from justice, and be found in another state, shall on demand of the executive authority of the state from which he fled, be delivered up, to be removed to the state having jurisdiction of the crime.

No person held to service or labor in one state, under the laws thereof, escaping into another, shall, in consequence of any law or regulation therein, be discharged from such service or labor, but shall be delivered up on claim of the party to whom such service or labor may be due.

Section 3. New states may be admitted by the Congress into this union; but no new states shall be formed or erected within the jurisdiction of any other state; nor any state be formed by the junction of two or more states, or parts of states, without the consent of the legislatures of the states concerned as well as of the Congress.

The Congress shall have power to dispose of and make all needful rules and regulations respecting the territory or other property belonging to the United States; and nothing in this Constitution shall be so construed as to prejudice any claims of the United States, or of any particular state.

Section 4. The United States shall guarantee to every state in this union a republican form of government, and shall protect each of them against invasion; and on application of the legislature, or of the executive (when the legislature cannot be convened) against domestic violence.

ARTICLE V

The Congress, whenever two thirds of both houses shall deem it necessary, shall propose amendments to this Constitution, or, on the application of the legislatures of two thirds of the several states, shall call a convention for proposing amendments, which, in either case, shall be valid to all intents and purposes, part of this Constitution, when ratified by the legislatures of three fourths of the several states, or by conventions in three fourths thereof, as the one or the other mode of ratification may be proposed by the Congress; provided that no amendment which may be made prior to the year one thousand eight hundred and eight shall in any manner affect the first and fourth clauses in the ninth section of the first article; and that no state, without its consent, shall be deprived of its equal suffrage in the Senate.

ARTICLE VI

All debts contracted and engagements entered into, before the adoption of this Constitution, shall be as valid against the United States under this Constitution, as under the Confederation.

This Constitution, and the laws of the United States which shall be made in pursuance thereof; and all treaties made, or which shall be made, under the authority of the United States, shall be the supreme law of the land; and the judges in every state shall be bound thereby, anything in the Constitution or laws of any State to the contrary notwithstanding.

The Senators and Representatives before mentioned, and the members of the several state legislatures, and all executive and judicial officers, both of the United States and of the several states, shall be bound by oath or affirmation, to support this Constitution; but no religious test shall ever be required as a qualification to any office or public trust under the United States.

ARTICLE VII

The ratification of the conventions of nine states, shall be sufficient for the establishment of this Constitution between the states so ratifying the same.

Done in convention by the unanimous consent of the states present the seventeenth day of September in the year of our Lord one thousand seven hundred and eighty seven and of the independence of the United States of America the twelfth. In witness whereof We have hereunto subscribed our Names,

G. Washington — Presidt. and deputy from Virginia
New Hampshire: John Langdon, Nicholas Gilman
Massachusetts: Nathaniel Gorham, Rufus King
Connecticut: Wm: Saml. Johnson, Roger Sherman
New York: Alexander Hamilton

New Jersey: Wil: Livingston, David Brearly, Wm. Paterson, Jona: Dayton

Pennsylvania: B. Franklin, Thomas Mifflin, Robt. Morris, Geo. Clymer, Thos. FitzSimons, Jared Ingersoll, James Wilson, Gouv Morris

Delaware: Geo: Read, Gunning Bedfordjun, John Dickinson, Richard Bassett, Jaco: Broom

Maryland: James McHenry, Dan of St. Thos. Jenifer, Danl Carroll

Virginia: John Blair — , James Madison Jr.

North Carolina: Wm. Blount, Richd. Dobbs Spaight, Hu Williamson

South Carolina: J. Rutledge, Charles Coteworth Pinckney, Charles Pinckney, Pierce Butler

Georgia: William Few, Abr Baldwin

The Bill of Rights

Amendments I–X of the Constitution

The Conventions of a number of the States having, at the time of adopting the Constitution, expressed a desire, in order to prevent misconstruction or abuse of its powers, that further declaratory and restrictive clauses should be added, and as extending the ground of public confidence in the Government will best insure the beneficent ends of its institution;

Resolved, by the Senate and House of Representatives of the United States of America, in Congress assembled, two-thirds of both Houses concurring, that the following articles be proposed to the Legislatures of the several States, as amendments to the Constitution of the United States; all or any of which articles, when ratified by three-fourths of the said Legislatures, to be valid to all intents and purposes as part of the said Constitution, namely:

Amendment I

Congress shall make no law respecting an establishment of religion, or prohibiting the free exercise thereof; or abridging the freedom of speech, or of the press; or the right of the people peaceably to assemble, and to petition the government for a redress of grievances.

Amendment II

A well regulated militia, being necessary to the security of a free state, the right of the people to keep and bear arms, shall not be infringed.

Amendment III

No soldier shall, in time of peace be quartered in any house, without the consent of the owner, nor in time of war, but in a manner to be prescribed by law.

Amendment IV

The right of the people to be secure in their persons, houses, papers, and effects, against unreasonable searches and seizures, shall not be violated, and no warrants shall issue, but upon probable cause, supported by oath or affirmation, and particularly describing the place to be searched, and the persons or things to be seized.

Amendment V

No person shall be held to answer for a capital, or otherwise infamous crime, unless on a presentment or indictment of a grand jury, except in cases arising in the land or naval forces, or in the militia, when in actual service in time of war or public danger; nor shall any person be subject for the same offense to be twice put in jeopardy of life or limb; nor shall be compelled in any criminal case to be a witness against himself, nor be deprived of life, liberty, or property, without due process of law; nor shall private property be taken for public use, without just compensation.

Amendment VI

In all criminal prosecutions, the accused shall enjoy the right to a speedy and public trial, by an impartial jury of the state and district wherein the crime shall have been committed, which district shall have been previously ascertained by law, and to be informed of the nature and cause of the accusation; to be confronted with the witnesses against him; to have compulsory process for obtaining witnesses in his favor, and to have the assistance of counsel for his defense.

Amendment VII

In suits at common law, where the value in controversy shall exceed twenty dollars, the right of trial by jury shall be preserved, and no fact tried by a jury, shall be otherwise reexamined in any court of the United States, than according to the rules of the common law.

Amendment VIII

Excessive bail shall not be required, nor excessive fines imposed, nor cruel and unusual punishments inflicted.

Amendment IX

The enumeration in the Constitution, of certain rights, shall not be construed to deny or disparage others retained by the people.

Amendment X

The powers not delegated to the United States by the Constitution, nor prohibited by it to the states, are reserved to the states respectively, or to the people.

Amendments to the Constitution

Amendment XI (1798)

The judicial power of the United States shall not be construed to extend to any suit in law or equity, commenced or prosecuted against one of the United States by citizens of another state, or by citizens or subjects of any foreign state.

Amendment XII (1804)

The electors shall meet in their respective states and vote by ballot for President and Vice-President, one of whom, at least, shall not be an inhabitant of the same state with themselves; they shall name in their ballots the person voted for as President, and in distinct ballots the person voted for as Vice-President, and they shall make distinct lists of all persons voted for as President, and of all persons voted for as Vice-President, and of the number of votes for each, which lists they shall sign and certify, and transmit sealed to the seat of the government of the United States, directed to the President of the Senate; — The President of the Senate shall, in the presence of the Senate and House of Representatives, open all the certificates and the votes shall then be counted; — the person having the greatest number of votes for President, shall be the President, if such number be a majority of the whole number of electors appointed; and if no person have such majority, then from the persons having the highest numbers not exceeding three on the list of those voted for as President, the House of Representatives shall choose immediately, by ballot, the President. But in choosing the President, the votes shall be taken by states, the representation from each state having one vote; a quorum for this purpose shall consist of a member or members from two-thirds of the states, and a majority of all the states shall be necessary to a choice. And if the House of Representatives shall not choose a President whenever the right of choice shall devolve upon them, before the fourth day of March next following, then the Vice-President shall act as President, as in the case of the death or other constitutional disability of the President. The person having the greatest number of votes as Vice-President, shall be the Vice-President, if such number be a majority of the whole number of electors appointed, and if no person have a majority, then from the two highest numbers on the list, the Senate shall choose the Vice-President; a quorum for the purpose shall consist of two-thirds of the whole number of Senators, and a majority of the whole number shall be necessary to a choice. But no person constitutionally ineligible to the office of President shall be eligible to that of Vice-President of the United States.

Amendment XIII (1865)

Section 1. Neither slavery nor involuntary servitude, except as a punishment for crime whereof the party shall have been duly convicted, shall exist within the United States, or any place subject to their jurisdiction.

Section 2. Congress shall have power to enforce this article by appropriate legislation.

Amendment XIV (1868)

Section 1. All persons born or naturalized in the United States, and subject to the jurisdiction thereof, are citizens of the United States and of the state wherein they reside. No state shall make or enforce any law which shall abridge the privileges or immunities of citizens of the United States; nor shall any state deprive any person of life, liberty, or property, without due process of law; nor deny to any person within its jurisdiction the equal protection of the laws.

Section 2. Representatives shall be apportioned among the several states according to their respective numbers, counting the whole number of persons in each state, excluding Indians not taxed. But when the right to vote at any election for the choice of electors for President and Vice President of the United States, Representatives in Congress, the executive and judicial officers of a state, or the members of the legislature thereof, is denied to any of the male inhabitants of such state, being twenty-one years of age, and citizens of the United States, or in any way abridged, except for participation in rebellion, or other crime, the basis of representation therein shall be reduced in the proportion which the number of such male citizens shall bear to the whole number of male citizens twenty-one years of age in such state.

Section 3. No person shall be a Senator or Representative in Congress, or elector of President and Vice President, or hold any office, civil or military, under the United States, or under any state, who, having previously taken an oath, as a member of Congress, or as an officer of the United States, or as a member of any state legislature, or as an executive or judicial officer of any state, to support the Constitution of the United States, shall have engaged in insurrection or rebellion against the same, or given aid or comfort to the enemies thereof. But Congress may by a vote of two-thirds of each House, remove such disability.

Section 4. The validity of the public debt of the United States, authorized by law, including debts incurred for payment of pensions and bounties for services in suppressing insurrection or rebellion, shall not be questioned. But neither the United States nor any state shall assume or pay any debt or obligation incurred in aid of insurrection or rebellion against the United States, or any claim for the loss or emancipation of any slave; but all such debts, obligations and claims shall be held illegal and void.

Section 5. The Congress shall have power to enforce, by appropriate legislation, the provisions of this article.

AMENDMENT XV (1870)

Section 1. The right of citizens of United States to vote shall not be denied or abridged by the United States or by any state on account of race, color, or previous condition of servitude.

Section 2. The Congress shall have power to enforce this article by appropriate legislation.

AMENDMENT XVI (1913)

The Congress shall have power to lay and collect taxes on incomes, from whatever source derived, without apportionment among the several states, and without regard to any census of enumeration.

AMENDMENT XVII (1913)

The Senate of the United States shall be composed of two Senators from each state, elected by the people thereof, for six years; and each Senator shall have one vote. The electors in each state shall have the qualifications requisite for electors of the most numerous branch of the state legislatures.

When vacancies happen in the representation of any state in the Senate, the executive authority of such state shall issue writs of election to fill such vacancies: Provided, that the legislature of any state may empower the executive thereof to make temporary appointments until the people fill the vacancies by election as the legislature may direct.

This amendment shall not be so construed as to affect the election or term of any Senator chosen before it becomes valid as part of the Constitution.

Amendment XVIII (1919)

Section 1. After one year from the ratification of this article the manufacture, sale, or transportation of intoxicating liquors within, the importation thereof into, or the exportation thereof from the United States and all territory subject to the jurisdiction thereof for beverage purposes is hereby prohibited.

Section 2. The Congress and the several states shall have concurrent power to enforce this article by appropriate legislation.

Section 3. This article shall be inoperative unless it shall have been ratified as an amendment to the Constitution by the legislatures of the several states, as provided in the Constitution, within seven years from the date of the submission hereof to the states by the Congress.

Amendment XIX (1920)

The right of citizens of the United States to vote shall not be denied or abridged by the United States or by any state on account of sex.

Congress shall have power to enforce this article by appropriate legislation.

Amendment XX (1933)

Section 1. The terms of the President and Vice President shall end at noon on the 20th day of January, and the terms of Senators and Representatives at noon on the 3d day of January, of the years in which such terms would have ended if this article had not been ratified; and the terms of their successors shall then begin.

Section 2. The Congress shall assemble at least once in every year, and such meeting shall begin at noon on the 3d day of January, unless they shall by law appoint a different day.

Section 3. If, at the time fixed for the beginning of the term of the President, the President elect shall have died, the Vice President elect shall become President. If a President shall not have been chosen before the time fixed for the beginning of his term, or if the President elect shall have failed to qualify, then the Vice President elect shall act as President until a President shall have qualified; and the Congress may by law provide for the case wherein neither a President elect nor a Vice President elect shall have qualified, declaring who shall then act as President, or the manner in which one who is to act shall be selected, and such person shall act accordingly until a President or Vice President shall have qualified.

Section 4. The Congress may by law provide for the case of the death of any of the persons from whom the House of Representatives may choose a President whenever the right of choice shall have devolved upon them, and for the case of the death of any of the persons from whom the Senate may choose a Vice President whenever the right of choice shall have devolved upon them.

Section 5. Sections 1 and 2 shall take effect on the 15th day of October following the ratification of this article.

Section 6. This article shall be inoperative unless it shall have been ratified as an amendment to the Constitution by the legislatures of three-fourths of the several states within seven years from the date of its submission.

Amendment XXI (1933)

Section 1. The eighteenth article of amendment to the Constitution of the United States is hereby repealed.

Section 2. The transportation or importation into any state, territory, or possession of the United States for delivery or use therein of intoxicating liquors, in violation of the laws thereof, is hereby prohibited.

Section 3. This article shall be inoperative unless it shall have been ratified as an amendment to the Constitution by conventions in the several states, as provided in the Constitution, within seven years from the date of the submission hereof to the states by the Congress.

Amendment XXII (1951)

Section 1. No person shall be elected to the office of the President more than twice, and no person who has held the office of President, or acted as President, for more than two years of a term to which some other person was elected President shall be elected to the office of the President more than once. But this article shall not apply to any person holding the office of President when this article was proposed by Congress, and shall not prevent any person who may be holding the office of President, or acting as President, during the term within which this article becomes operative from holding the office of President or acting as President during the remainder of such term.

Section 2. This article shall be inoperative unless it shall have been ratified as an amendment to the Constitution by the legislatures of three-fourths of the several states within seven years from the date of its submission to the states by the Congress.

AMENDMENT XXIII (1961)

Section 1. The District constituting the seat of government of the United States shall appoint in such manner as the Congress may direct:

A number of electors of President and Vice President equal to the whole number of Senators and Representatives in Congress to which the District would be entitled if it were a state, but in no event more than the least populous state; they shall be in addition to those appointed by the states, but they shall be considered, for the purposes of the election of President and Vice President, to be electors appointed by a state; and they shall meet in the District and perform such duties as provided by the twelfth article of amendment.

Section 2. The Congress shall have power to enforce this article by appropriate legislation.

AMENDMENT XXIV (1964)

Section 1. The right of citizens of the United States to vote in any primary or other election for President or Vice President, for electors for President or Vice President, or for Senator or Representative in Congress, shall not be denied or abridged by the United States or any state by reason of failure to pay any poll tax or other tax.

Section 2. The Congress shall have power to enforce this article by appropriate legislation.

Amendment XXV (1967)

Section 1. In case of the removal of the President from office or of his death or resignation, the Vice President shall become President.

Section 2. Whenever there is a vacancy in the office of the Vice President, the President shall nominate a Vice President who shall take office upon confirmation by a majority vote of both Houses of Congress.

Section 3. Whenever the President transmits to the President pro tempore of the Senate and the Speaker of the House of Representatives his written declaration that he is unable to discharge the powers and duties of his office, and until he transmits to them a written declaration to the contrary, such powers and duties shall be discharged by the Vice President as Acting President.

Section 4. Whenever the Vice President and a majority of either the principal officers of the executive departments or of such other body as Congress may by law provide, transmit to the President pro tempore of the Senate and the Speaker of the House of Representatives their written declaration that the President is unable to discharge the powers and duties of his office, the Vice President shall immediately assume the powers and duties of the office as Acting President.

Thereafter, when the President transmits to the President pro tempore of the Senate and the Speaker of the House of Representatives his written declaration that no inability exists, he shall resume the powers and duties of his office unless the Vice President and a majority of either the principal officers of the executive department or of such other body as Congress may by law provide, transmit within four days to the President pro tempore of the Senate and the Speaker of the House of Representatives their written declaration that the President is unable to discharge the powers and duties of his office. Thereupon Congress shall decide the issue, assembling within forty-eight hours for that purpose if not in session. If the Congress, within twenty-one days after receipt of the latter written declaration, or, if Congress is not in session, within twenty-one days after Congress is required to assemble, determines by two-thirds vote of both Houses that the President is unable to discharge the powers and duties of his office, the Vice President shall continue to discharge the same as Acting President; otherwise, the President shall resume the powers and duties of his office.

Amendment XXVI (1971)

Section 1. The right of citizens of the United States, who are 18 years of age or older, to vote, shall not be denied or abridged by the United States or any state on account of age.

Section 2. The Congress shall have the power to enforce this article by appropriate legislation.

Amendment XXVII (1992)

No law varying the compensation for the services of the Senators and Representatives shall take effect until an election of Representatives shall have intervened.

– – – –

Editor's Note: The originals of these, and other U.S. historical documents, can be viewed at The National Archives (National Archives and Records Administration) Building, located at 700 Pennsylvania Avenue, N.W., Washington, D.C. 20408, telephone (866) 325-7208, or purchased through their website (http://www.nara.gov/).

Notes

1. The U.S. Department of Veterans Affairs was established as a Cabinet-level position by Congress on March 15, 1989. Since the date of this chapter is 1987, the information about this new federal department was added to this chapter to make it as accurate as possible. Much of this information was obtained from the Department of Veterans Affairs Home Page (http://www.va.gov/).

2. These copies of *The U.S. Constitution*, *The Bill of Rights*, and *Amendments to the Constitution* were obtained from Thomas Legislative Information, Library of Congress, 101 Independence Avenue, S.E., Washington, D.C. 20540, telephone (202) 707-5000, and can be downloaded from their website (http://www.loc.gov/).

Glossary

Following is a list of terms commonly used to describe city, county, regional, state, and federal governments, and the actions taken by their public officials.

Abolish   To do away with; to put an end to.

Act   Legislation which has passed both Houses of Congress, approved by the President, or passed over his veto, thus becoming law. Also used technically for a bill that has been passed by one House and engrossed.

Adjourn   To stop or interrupt a meeting or session for a certain length of time.

Amendment   A proposal by a Member (in committee or floor session of the respective Chamber) to alter the language or provisions of a bill or act. It is voted on in the same manner as a bill.

Appeal   A request for a new hearing with a higher court.

Appellate Court   A court which has the power to hear **appeals** and reverse court decisions.

Appointed Officials   Public officials appointed by elected officials. These officials typically include an organization's top management staff (that is, chief executive and department managers).

Appointment   An office or position for which one is chosen, not elected.

Appropriation   A formal approval to draw funds from the Treasury for specific purposes. This may occur through an annual appropriations act, an urgent or supplemental appropriations act, a continuing resolution, or on a permanent basis.

At-large Elections   An election system where candidates are elected on a city-wide basis.

Authorization   A law creating or sustaining a program, delegating power to implement it, and outlining its funding. Following authorization, an appropriation actually draws funds from the Treasury.

Bill   A proposed law which is being considered for approval.

Bipartisanship   Cooperation between Members of both political parties in addressing a particular issue or proposal. Bipartisan action usually results when party leaders agree that an issue is of sufficient national importance as to preclude normal considerations of partisan advantage.

Board of Supervisors   Typical name for the members of a governing body of a county.

Boards and Commissions   Typical names given to advisory bodies, appointed by the members of a governing body, to advise them on matters of importance in one of the many functional areas of government.

Calendar   A list of bills, resolutions, or other matters to be considered before committees or on the floor of either House of Congress.

Campaign   An attempt to convince people to vote for someone for public office.

Candidate   A person seeking to obtain an office or position.

Census   An official count of the population.

Charter   A written grant which establishes a local government corporation or other institution, and defines its purposes and privileges.

Checks and Balances   System of government which maintains balance of power among the branches of the government. Sets limits on the power of each branch. Sets up ways for each branch to correct any misuses of power by the other branches.

Citizen Participation   Strategies have greater legitimacy and are easier to implement politically when the citizens served by a governmental entity feel that their interests and issues have been properly addressed during the planning process.

City Council   Typical name for the members of a governing body of a municipality.

City Manager   The Chief Executive Officer of a municipality.

Civil   Relating to the rights of individuals, such as property and personal freedoms. Also, court cases which are not **criminal**.

Civil Rights   Rights which belong to a person because of his or her being a member of a particular society, for example, an American.

Combination Elections   A hybrid election system where some candidates are elected on a city-wide basis, while other candidates are elected from a district, or ward.

Committee   A group of people officially chosen to investigate or discuss a particular issue.

Compromise   To settle differences by accepting less than what was wanted.

Constraint   Limitation; restriction.

Contradict   To conflict with; to oppose.

Controversial   Relating to issues about which people have and express opposing views.

Cost/Benefit Analysis   The relationship between economic benefits and costs associated with the operation of the department or program under study. The cost/benefit analysis may include both direct and indirect benefits and costs. Such analyses typically result in a payback period on initial investment.

Cost Center   The smallest practical breakdown of expenditure and income into a grouping which will facilitate performance review, service evaluation, and the setting of priorities for a particular activity or service area. Typically it includes a portion of a single program within a department.

County Manager   The Chief Executive Officer of a county government.

Cross Impact Analysis   An analytical technique for identifying the various impacts of specific events or well-defined policy actions on other events. It explores whether the occurrence of one event or implementation of one policy is likely to inhibit, enhance, or have no effect on the occurrence of another event.

Criminal   Relating to court cases in which a person has been accused of committing an action that is harmful to the public, such as murder or burglary.

Debate   To discuss reasons for and against an issue or idea.

Delegate   To grant or assign responsibility to another; to authorize a person or persons to represent the rest of the people.

Direct Democracy   The people vote to make all of the decisions about their government.

Discrimination   Being treated differently, usually worse, for some characteristic such as race, religion, national origin or sex. Discrimination is discouraged in the U.S.

District Elections   An election system where candidates are elected from a district, or ward.

Econometric Model   Forecasting technique that involves a system of interdependent regression equations that describe some sector of economic sales or profit activity. The parameters of the regression equations are usually estimated simultaneously. This technique better expresses the causalities involved than an ordinary regression equation.

Effectiveness   Performing the right tasks correctly, consistent with a program's mission, goals, and objectives, or work plan. Relates to correctness and accuracy, not the efficiency of the program or tasks performed. Effectiveness alone is not an accurate measure of total productivity.

Efficiency   Operating a program or performing work tasks economically. Relates to dollars spent or saved, not to the effectiveness of the program or task performed. Efficiency alone is not an accurate measure of total productivity.

Elected Officials   Those public officials that hold elective office for a specified time period, typically called a term of office.

Environmental Scanning   Process of identifying major environmental factors, events, or trends that impact, directly or indirectly, the organization and its internal operating systems. It is one of the initial steps in undertaking a strategic planning process.

Evaluation   Systematic review of the mission, goals, objectives, and work plan for the organization and its various components. Evaluation occurs most frequently at the operational level by reviewing organizational objectives. The evaluation process typically results in the preparation of recommendations for needed adjustments.

Executive   Person or group of persons responsible for governmental affairs and enforcement of laws.

Executive Director   The title frequently used for the Chief Executive Officer of a regional government agency.

Exempt   Free or excused from a requirement or duty.

External Environment   All relevant elements or forces (for example, social, economic, political, and technological) external to, and having an impact on, the organization and its various components. Includes those forces that are not under the direct control of management.

Forecasting Techniques   Methods (for example, qualitative, quantitative, and causal) used to project trends and predict future events or courses of action. Forecasting is an essential component of the strategic planning process. It may be used to analyze the external environment or to project organizational capabilities.

Foreign Policy   The way a country treats and relates to the other countries of the world.

Forms of County Government   Major forms include Commission, Commission-Administrator, and Council-Executive.

Forms of Municipal Government   Major forms include Council-Manager, Mayor-Council, Commission, and Strong Mayor.

General Election   A voting process involving most or all areas of the nation or state.

General Purpose Local Governments   Includes cities and counties, since they both provide a wide range of services to the citizens they serve.

Gerrymandering   Drawing of district lines to maximize the electoral advantage of a political party or faction. The term was first used in 1812, when Elbridge Gerry was Governor of Massachusetts, to characterize the State redistricting plan.

Governor   The Chief Executive Officer of a state government.

Hierarchical   Ordered by rank or authority.

Hierarchy   The order in which authority is ranked.

Impeach   To charge a public official with committing a crime.

Inaugurate   To place in office by a formal ceremony.

Influence   The power to produce or cause an effect; to have an effect upon.

Inherent Rights   Essential, basic rights.

Intergovernmental Relations   The relationships between public officials at the various levels of government, most often dictated by legislation (e.g., grant requirements).

Internal Environment   Relevant elements or forces (e.g., personnel, financial, communications, authority relationships, and management operating systems) internal to, and having an impact on, the operation of the organization and its various components. Includes those forces that are under the direct control of management.

Issue   Trend, set of elements, or event which a group decides is important for policy-making purposes.

Issues Management   Attempt to manage those issues that are important to an organization. These issues typically surface after the completion of an environmental scanning process, or other practice, leading to the identification of important issues. The issues identified should fall within the scope and purpose of the organization.

Jury   A group of people chosen to hear a case in court. The *jury* makes a decision based upon the evidence.

Lame Duck Session   A session of Congress meeting after elections have been held, but before the newly elected Congress has convened.

Law   In municipal and county government this takes the form of an ordinance, which must be passed by majority vote of the governing body and published in a newspaper of general circulation.

Legislation   The act or procedure of making laws; a law or laws made by such a procedure.

Levy   To collect, a tax, for example.

Life-Cycle Analysis   Involves an analysis and forecasting of new product or service growth rates based on S-curves. The phases of product or service acceptance by various groups are central to this analytical technique.

Line   Personnel in those departments charged with the responsibility for those functions necessary for the day-to-day performance of the organization. Includes those departments that directly produce goods and/or services to satisfy an organization's marketplace.

Line of Succession   Order to **succession**.

Long-Range Planning   Includes a planning process that commences with analyzing the internal organization and projecting current trends into the future for selected organizational components. This planning process may not include an assessment of an organization's external environment. It may be product or service oriented. This term should not be confused with strategic planning.

Management   Consists basically of two types—strategic and operational. Strategic management is performed at the top of an organization's hierarchy; everything else is operational management. Operational management is organized along functional lines of responsibility. Strategic management sets direction for the organization, and operational management ensures that this direction is implemented.

Management Information System   Integrated information system designed to provide strategic, tactical, and operational information to management. Usually involves periodic written or computer-generated reports which are timely, concise, and meaningful.

Management Operating System   Formal system of linkages between different components of the organization by which the various departments communicate with each other and by which management directs the operation and receives information on its performance.

Mayor   Typical name for the highest elective office in a municipality.

Mission   Statement of the role, or purpose, by which an organization plans to serve society. Mission statements may be set for different organizational components or departments. A department usually has only one mission statement.

Municipal   The smallest unit of local government in the U.S.

Negotiate   To discuss and then **compromise** on an issue to reach an agreement.

Nonprofit Organization   Sometimes referred to as the third sector — the other two being the public and private sectors. Nonprofit organizations generally serve a public purpose and do not generate revenues beyond their operating expenses.

Objectives   Tasks which are deemed necessary for an organization, or its components and departments, to achieve its goals. Several detailed objectives are typically set forth for each goal statement. Objectives include the operational implementation of goals.

Operational Issues   Issues that relate to the internal operations of an organization such as finance, budgeting, personnel, and technology, to name a few. Operational issues may or may not relate to an organization's external environment and may not be of strategic importance to an organization.

Operational Management   Tasks performed by line managers dealing with the operations of the organization. Operational managers may provide input into the formulation of strategic plans, but such plans are formulated by the planning group. Operational managers are key actors in implementing components of strategic plans.

Opponent   Person who ran against others in an election for an office or a position.

Opportunity Cost   Cost of not taking a particular course of action. For example, if there are two issues and one is deemed to be strategic and the other is not, then the opportunity cost is the cost of not pursuing the course of action required for the nonstrategic issue. If the purchase of computers is a strategic issue, and the cost to purchase typewriters is not, then the cost of not acquiring the typewriters is an opportunity cost.

Override   To nullify; to pass over.

Pardon   To forgive a person for something he/she did wrong; to release or free a person from punishment.

Petition   A formal request, usually written, for a right or benefit from a person or group with authority.

Philosophy   The general beliefs, attitudes and ideas or theories of a person or group.

Platform   The stated principles of a **candidate** for public office or a political party.

Policy   Chosen course of action designed to significantly affect the organization's behavior in prescribed situations.

Political Action Committee (PAC)   A group organized to promote its members' views on selected issues, usually through raising money that is contributed to the campaign funds of candidates who support the group's position.

President   The Chief Executive Officer of the federal government organization.

Productivity   Measure of performance that includes the requirements of both efficiency and effectiveness. Includes performing the program or work tasks correctly (effectively) and economically (efficiently).

Pro Tempore   For the time being; temporarily.

Preliminary   Introductory; something that comes before and is necessary to what follows.

Preside   To hold the position of authority; to be in charge of a meeting or group.

Primary Election   Election by which the **candidate** who will represent a particular political party is chosen.

Ratification   Two uses of this term are: (1) the act of approval of a proposed constitutional amendment by the legislatures of the States; (2) the Senate process of advice and consent to treaties negotiated by the President.

Ratify   To approve or confirm formally; to make valid and binding.

Redistricting   The process within the States of redrawing legislative district boundaries to reflect population changes following the decennial census.

Regional Government   A multi-jurisdictional agency that includes any combination of cities and counties, and is usually sub-state in nature. Only a few regional governments involve more than one state.

Regulation   Rule or order which controls actions and procedures.

Repeal   To take back or recall, usually a law.

Representative Democracy   The people choose or elect officials to make decisions for them about their government. On some issues, however, the people vote, rather than their representatives.

Republican   Democratic; representative.

Resolution   A legislative act without the force of law, such as action taken to adopt a policy or to modify an existing program.

Ruling   The official decision of a court on the case being tried.

Sentence   Judgment or decision; usually a decision on the punishment for a person convicted of a crime.

Special Purpose Local Governments   Includes special districts, which perform a single public service or function (e.g., water, sewer, and transportation districts, to name a few).

Staff   Personnel in those departments designed to serve the operating components, or line departments, of an organization (e.g., personnel, finance, general services, purchasing, etc.).

Stakeholder   Those individuals, groups, and outside parties that either affect or who are affected by the organization. Examples include constituents, special-interest groups, suppliers, unions, employees, policy-makers, and advisory bodies, to name a few. In any strategic planning process these entities must either be involved or consulted so that their views are given consideration during the planning process.

Strategic Issues   Issues included in a strategic plan which are deemed important to the organization and its future performance. These issues may be either internal or external to the organization itself. Typically external issues are more difficult to manage than internal issues, due to the limited degree of control exercised by public organizations over their outside environment.

Strategic Management   Involves setting direction for the organization and is typically performed by elected and appointed officials, or some combination of these individuals, once a strategic plan is approved for implementation. While the strategic plan is approved by elected officials, top management is responsible for its administrative implementation.

Strategic Vision   Explicit, shared understanding of the nature and purpose of the organization. It specifies what the organization is and should be rather than what it does operationally. The strategic vision is contained within an organization's strategy statement.

Strategy   General direction set for the organization and its various components to achieve a desired state in the future. Strategy results from the detailed planning process that assesses the external and internal environment of an organization and results in a work plan that includes mission statements to direct the goals and objectives of the organization.

Structure   Segmentation of work into components, typically organized around those goods and services produced, the formal lines of authority and communication between these components, and the information that flows between these communication and authority relationships.

Succession   Order in which one person follows another in replacing a person in an office or position.

Table   To postpone or delay making a decision on an issue or law.

Time Horizon   A timespan included in a plan, or planning document, varies depending on the type of plan being developed. Strategic plans typically have a five or ten year, sometimes longer, time horizon. Operational plans, on the other hand, frequently project a three to five year timespan into the future.

Unconstitutional   In conflict with a constitution.

Veto   Power of the head of the **executive** branch to keep a bill from becoming law.

– – – –

Editor's Note: Some of the above terms were taken from *U.S. Government Structure* (1987), and *Our American Government* (1993), U.S. Government Printing Office, Washington, D.C. Copies of these books may be obtained from the U.S. Government Printing Office, P.O. Box 371954, Pittsburgh, Pennsylvania 15250-7954, or may be ordered over the internet from GPO's online bookstore (http://bookstore.gpo.gov).

National Resource
Directory

*Major national professional associations and research organizations
serving city, county, regional, state and federal government*

Alliance for National Renewal
c/o National Civic League
1319 "F" Street, N.W.
Suite 204
Washington, D.C. 20004
Telephone: (202) 783-2961
FAX: (202) 347-2161
http://www.ncl.org/anr

**Alliance for Redesigning
  Government**
c/o National Academy of Public
  Administration
1100 New York Avenue, N.W.
Suite 1090 East
Washington, D.C. 20005
Telephone: (202) 347-3190
FAX: (202) 393-0993
http://www.alliance.napawash.org

Alliance for Regional Stewardship
785 Castro Street
Suite A
Mountain View, CA 94011

Telephone: (650) 623-3082
FAX: (650) 623-0900
http://www.regionalstewardship.org

American Planning Association
122 South Michigan Avenue
Suite 1600
Chicago, IL 60603-6107
Telephone: (312) 431-9100
FAX: (312) 431-9985
http://www.planning.org

**American Society for Public
  Administration**
1120 "G" Street, N.W.
Suite 700
Washington, D.C. 20005
Telephone: (202) 393-7878
FAX: (202) 638-4952
http://www.aspanet.org

**Center for Regional and
  Neighborhood Action**
1009 Grant Street

Suite 203
Denver, CO 80203
Telephone: (303) 477-9985
FAX: (303) 477-9986
http://www.crna.net

Council of State Governments
P.O. Box 11910
Lexington, KY 40578-1910
Telephone: (859) 244-8105
FAX: (859) 244-8001
http://www.csg.org

Government Finance Officers Association
180 North Michigan Avenue
Suite 800
Chicago, IL 60601
Telephone: (312) 977-9700
FAX: (312) 977-4806
http://www.gfoa.org

International City/County Management Association
777 North Capitol Street, N.E.
Suite 500
Washington, D.C. 20002
Telephone: (202) 289-4262
FAX: (202) 962-3500
http://www.icma.org

Library of Congress
Thomas Legislative Information
101 Independence Avenue, S.E.
Washington, D.C. 20540
Telephone: (202) 707-5000
FAX: (202) 707-2777
http://www.loc.gov

National Academy of Public Administration
1101 New York Avenue
Suite 1090 East
Washington, D.C. 20005
Telephone: (202) 347-3190
FAX: (202) 393-0993
http://www.napawash.org

National Archives and Records Administration
The National Archives
700 Pennsylvania Avenue, N.W.
Washington, D.C. 20048
Telephone: (866) 325-7208
FAX: (301) 713-6913
http://www.nara.gov

National Association of Attorneys General
750 First Street, N.E.
Suite 1100
Washington, D.C. 20002
Telephone: (202) 326-6000
FAX: (202) 408-7014
http://www.naag.org

National Association of Counties
440 First Street, N.W.
Washington, D.C. 20001-2080
Telephone: (202) 393-6226
FAX: (202) 393-2630
http://www.naco.org

National Association of Regional Councils
1700 "K" Street
Suite 1300
Washington, D.C. 20006
Telephone: (202) 457-0710
FAX: (202) 296-9352
http://www.narc.org

National Civic League
1445 Market Street
Suite 300
Denver, CO 80202-1728
Telephone: (303) 571-4343
FAX: (303) 571-4404
http://www.ncl.org

National Conference of Commissioners on Uniform State Laws
211 E. Ontario Street
Suite 1300
Chicago, IL 60611

Telephone: (312) 915-0195
FAX: (312) 915-0187
http://www.nccusl.org

**National Conference of State
  Legislatures**
444 North Capitol Street, N.W.
Suite 515
Washington, D.C. 20001
Telephone: (202) 624-5400
FAX: (202) 737-1069
http://www.ncsl.org

**National Institute of Municipal Law
  Officers**
1000 Connecticut Avenue, N.W.
Suite 902
Washington, D.C. 20136
Telephone: (202) 466-5424
FAX: (202) 785-0152
http://www.imla.org

National League of Cities
1301 Pennsylvania Avenue, N.W.
Washington, D.C. 20004-1763
Telephone: (202) 626-3000
FAX: (202) 626-3043
http://www.nlc.org

Partnership for Regional Livability
2125 West North Avenue
Chicago, IL 60647
Telephone: (773) 278-4800, Ext. 135
FAX: (773) 278-3840
http://www.pfrl.org

United States Conference of Mayors
1620 Eye Street, N.W.
4th Floor
Washington, D.C. 20006
Telephone: (202) 293-7330
FAX: (202) 293-2352
http://www.usmayors.org

U.S. Government Printing Office
Federal Building, Room 118
1000 Liberty Avenue
Pittsburgh, PA 15222
Telephone: (412) 395-5021
FAX: (412) 395-4547
http://bookstore.gpo.gov

The Urban Institute
2100 "M" Street, N.W.
Washington, D.C. 20037
Telephone: (202) 833-7200
FAX: (202) 331-9747
http://www.urban.org

About the Contributors

Affiliations are as of the time the articles were written.

Victor S. DeSantis, Associate Professor, Department of Political Science, Bridgewater State College, Bridgewater, Massachusetts.

Christopher T. Gates, President, National Civil League, Denver, Colorado.

Frank P. Grad, Director, Legislative Drafting Research Fund, Columbia University, New York, New York.

Roger L. Kemp, Author, Editor, Futurist, and City Manager, Meriden, Connecticut.

Bruce D. McDowell, Director of Government Policy Research, U.S. Advisory Commission on Intergovernmental Relations, Washington, D.C.

Edwin Meese, III, former Attorney General, Department of Justice, U.S. Federal Government, Washington, D.C.

Metro Charter Committee, Metropolitan Service District, Portland, Oregon.

John Parr, President, National Civic League, Denver, Colorado.

Index